Words for Weeks 1-

Week 1
subject
topic

Week 2
edit
revise
revision

Week 3
usual
unusual
regular

Week 4
brief
abbreviate
abbreviation
pause

Week 5
define
definition
definite
definitely

Week 6
increase
decrease

Week 7
form
format
style

Week 8
conclude
conclusion

subject
DAY 1

(noun) An area of study, such as science.

*Math is Greta's best **subject** in school.*

subject
DAY 2

(noun) Someone or something that is thought about, written about, or talked about.

*Our school picnic was the **subject** of a newspaper article.*

topic
DAY 3

(noun) The subject of discussion or conversation.

*Abigail always has lots to say on the **topic** of dog care.*

topic
DAY 4

(noun) The subject of a book or other written work.

*He has read many books on the **topic** of space travel.*

Day 1 subject

1. How would you complete this sentence? Say it aloud to a partner.

My idea of a hard subject is ________.

2. Which of these is not a *subject* you study in school? Circle your answer.

a. math
b. spelling
c. bike riding
d. science

3. In what *subject* would you study each of these things? Draw lines to match.

a. the solar system	math
b. subtraction	science
c. our country's history	writing
d. nouns and verbs	social studies

Day 2 subject

1. How would you complete this sentence? Say it aloud to a partner.

My favorite books are on the subject of ________.

2. The title of a book is What's Out There: A Book About Space. What is the *subject* of this book? Circle your answer.

a. backyards
b. empty rooms
c. outer space
d. woods and meadows

3. List three *subjects* that interest you.

a. ______________________________

b. ______________________________

c. ______________________________

Day 3 topic

1. How would you complete this sentence? Say it aloud to a partner.

I could say a lot about the topic of ______.

2. Which of these *topics* would you talk about in science class? Circle your answers.

a. how magnets work
b. a favorite TV show
c. how plants grow
d. nouns and verbs

3. Which sentence correctly uses the word *topic*? Circle your answer.

a. They hiked to the topic of the mountain.
b. They talked about a different topic every night.
c. I like to topic about my favorite book.
d. She took a topic to avoid getting the flu.

Day 4 topic

1. How would you complete this sentence? Say it aloud to a partner.

I would be interested in an article on the topic of ______.

2. Which of these would make a good *topic* for a science report? Circle your answer.

a. how I spent my summer vacation
b. how a caterpillar becomes a butterfly
c. how the president is elected
d. how to make a turkey sandwich

3. Pretend that you are going to write a report. First, write the *topic* of your report. Then, write three things you would say about the *topic.*

Topic: My Dog

a. He likes to chase balls.
b. He has a big wet tongue.
c. He sleeps on my bed.

Topic: ______________________

a. ______________________

b. ______________________

c. ______________________

Day 5 subject • topic

Fill in the bubble next to the correct answer.

1. Which sentence could you complete with the word *subject*?

Ⓐ We have a different textbook for every ________.

Ⓑ Grandma's barn was the ________ for Barney's doghouse.

Ⓒ The librarian is a good ________ to help you find a book.

Ⓓ The dinosaur was ________ in the museum.

2. The *subject* of a book is ________.

Ⓕ a list of the chapters

Ⓖ a list of the topics covered in the book

Ⓗ what the book is about

Ⓙ the person who wrote the book

3. In which sentence could you replace the underlined word with the word *topic*?

Ⓐ A birthday is a good <u>reason</u> for celebration.

Ⓑ For some players, winning is the <u>object</u> of the game.

Ⓒ The dinner table is the perfect <u>place</u> for conversation.

Ⓓ Movies are Emma's favorite <u>subject</u> for discussion.

4. What is the *topic* of a news article entitled "California Feels the Heat"?

Ⓕ unusually cold weather in California

Ⓖ wood-burning stoves

Ⓗ hot weather in California

Ⓙ hot weather in Mexico

Writing Tell about the *subject* of a book you have read lately. Be sure to use the word *subject* in your writing.

____

____

____

edit
DAY 1

(verb) To check and correct errors in writing.

*Before he handed it in, Rosemary **edited** Andrew's story.*

revise
DAY 2

(verb) To make a piece of writing better by making it clearer or more correct.

*The reporter will **revise** the newspaper article to include the new information.*

revision
DAY 3

(noun) A change that makes something better.

*The **revisions** in word choice improved my sentences.*

revise
DAY 4

(verb) To change or make different.

*He **revised** his plans when he saw the rain.*

Day 1 edit

1. How would you complete this sentence? Say it aloud to a partner.

It's important to edit your work to ________.

2. Which of the following things would you *edit?* Circle your answers.

a. a book report you wrote
b. a picture you painted
c. a model you built
d. a story you wrote

3. Which things might you do when you *edit?* Circle your answers.

a. write the first sentence
b. add a comma
c. correct a misspelled word
d. tape a torn page

Day 2 revise

1. How would you complete this sentence? Say it aloud to a partner.

When you revise a story that you wrote, you ________.

2. Why would you *revise* a book report? Circle your answers.

a. You are bored.
b. You forgot an important part.
c. You wrote the wrong title.
d. You want to type it on the computer.

3. Which sentence correctly uses the word *revise?* Circle your answer.

a. We will revise the computer.
b. We will revise the old house with paint.
c. We will revise the book to include new information.
d. We will revise what we learned to get ready for the test.

Day 3 revision

1. How would you complete this sentence? Say it aloud to a partner.

I might make a revision to ______ because ______.

2. Which of the following is not an example of a *revision*? Circle your answer.

a. adding new information
b. adding a new sentence
c. learning a poem by heart
d. changing the order of words in a sentence

3. Which word has the same meaning as *revision*? Circle your answer.

a. review
b. change
c. memory
d. copy

Day 4 revise

1. How would you complete this sentence? Say it aloud to a partner.

Once my family had to revise our plans to ______.

2. In which sentence does someone *revise* something? Circle your answers.

a. Sari would not listen to her friend.
b. John changed his mind when he heard Jason's side of the story.
c. Maria studied for her test.
d. Angel wrote a story to read to the class.

3. Which phrase best completes this sentence? Circle your answer.

I revised my idea when ______.

a. I kept it the same
b. I fell asleep
c. I thought of something better
d. I read about it

Day 5 edit • revise • revision

Fill in the bubble next to the correct answer.

1. Which sentence uses the word *edit* correctly?

Ⓐ Always edit your pencil.

Ⓑ Please edit your report before handing it in.

Ⓒ Jeremy will edit the map to find out where we are.

Ⓓ I will edit the paragraph by writing it neatly.

2. When you *revise* something, you ________.

Ⓕ make it clearer or more correct

Ⓖ show your work

Ⓗ copy it exactly as it was written

Ⓙ read it out loud

3. In which sentence could *revision* be used to fill in the blank?

Ⓐ She will ________ her last paragraph.

Ⓑ This picture is a ________ of a famous painting.

Ⓒ The new book is a ________ of a book written ten years ago.

Ⓓ Always ________ your stories.

4. In which sentence could the underlined word <u>not</u> be replaced by *revise*?

Ⓕ We need to <u>update</u> our thinking.

Ⓖ You could <u>rethink</u> your views on the story.

Ⓗ The plan is perfect, and we don't need to <u>change</u> it.

Ⓙ Parents sometimes <u>preview</u> the movies their children want to see.

Writing Think about something you wrote for class recently. What is one thing you did to *revise* it? Be sure to use the word *revise* in your writing.

____

____

____

usual
DAY 1

(adj.) Normal, common, or expected.

*We did the **usual** things that we do every day.*

unusual
DAY 2

(adj.) Not usual or ordinary.

*It is very **unusual** for it to snow in Alabama.*

regular
DAY 3

(adj.) Usual or normal.

*Vegetables should be a **regular** part of everyone's diet.*

regular
DAY 4

(adj.) Always happening at the same time.

*This bus makes **regular** trips to the library.*

Day 1 usual

1. How would you complete this sentence? Say it aloud to a partner.

The usual things I do after dinner are ________.

2. Which of the following are *usual* activities at your school? Circle your answers.

a. Teachers play on the swings.
b. Students read books.
c. The principal runs in the halls.
d. Students draw pictures and do art projects.

3. Which two words have about the same meaning as *usual*? Circle your answers.

a. common
b. strange
c. normal
d. helpful

Day 2 unusual

1. How would you complete this sentence? Say it aloud to a partner.

It would be unusual to see ________ at school.

2. Which of these animals would make an *unusual* pet? Circle your answer.

a. cat
b. dog
c. bear
d. hamster

3. List three things that are usual things to see at a library and three things that would be *unusual.*

Usual	Unusual
a. ____________	a. ____________
b. ____________	b. ____________
c. ____________	c. ____________

Day 3 regular

1. How would you complete this sentence? Say it aloud to a partner.

One of my regular chores is ________.

2. Which of these words means the opposite of *regular*? Circle your answer.

a. normal c. usual
b. special d. common

3. List three activities that are *regular* parts of your school day.

a. ______________________________

b. ______________________________

c. ______________________________

Day 4 regular

1. How would you complete this sentence? Say it aloud to a partner.

We have regular ________ at school.

2. Which of the following things might be *regular*? Circle your answers.

a. visits to the library c. trips to the supermarket
b. winning one million dollars d. your ninth birthday

3. Which group of words best completes this sentence? Circle your answer.

Dentists want their patients to have regular ________.

a. sweets and desserts
b. afternoon naps
c. vacations at the beach
d. teeth cleanings

Day 5 usual • unusual • regular

Fill in the bubble next to the correct answer.

1. In which sentence could *usual* take the place of the underlined word?

Ⓐ Field Day was a <u>special</u> day for everyone.
Ⓑ We did not follow our <u>everyday</u> activities.
Ⓒ We learned lots of <u>new</u> games and fun activities.
Ⓓ The day was very <u>different</u> and out of the ordinary.

2. Which word has the same meaning as *unusual*?

Ⓕ normal
Ⓖ unexpected
Ⓗ common
Ⓙ regular

3. In which sentence is the word *regular* <u>not</u> used correctly?

Ⓐ Feeding the cat was one of her regular chores.
Ⓑ The regular visitor had never been there before.
Ⓒ The children got to stay up past their regular bedtime.
Ⓓ Reading and writing are part of our regular classroom routine.

4. We have *regular* practice ________.

Ⓕ on different days each week
Ⓖ at different times each week
Ⓗ at the same time each week
Ⓙ whenever our coach thinks we need it

Writing Describe something *unusual* that happened to you.
Be sure to use the word *unusual* in your writing.

____

____

____

brief DAY 1

(adj.) Short in time or length.

*She left a **brief** message on the answering machine.*

abbreviate DAY 2

(verb) To shorten the time or length of something.

*Because the baby was restless, his mother **abbreviated** their visit to Grandma's.*

abbreviate • abbreviation DAY 3

abbreviate

(verb) To shorten a word by leaving out letters.

*You can **abbreviate** the word "Street" to "St."*

---

abbreviation

(noun) A shortened form of a word or phrase used in writing.

*The **abbreviation** for Maine is ME.*

pause DAY 4

(noun) A short stop or rest.

*The period at the end of the sentence signals a **pause**.*

(verb) To stop for a short time in the middle of something.

*When reading aloud, you should **pause** at commas and periods.*

Day 1 brief

1. How would you complete this sentence? Say it aloud to a partner.

I could give a brief talk on the subject of ________.

2. Which words have about the same meaning as *brief*? Circle your answers.

a. short
b. lengthy
c. stretched out
d. quick

3. Which of the following would you call *brief*? Circle your answers.

a. a good night's sleep
b. a nap
c. a 100-page book
d. a telephone message

Day 2 abbreviate

1. How would you complete this sentence? Say it aloud to a partner.

A speaker might decide to abbreviate her speech because ________.

2. Which phrase best completes this sentence? Circle your answer.

When you abbreviate something, you ________.

a. take away pain
b. provide more information
c. make it shorter
d. make it clearer and more complete

3. Why would something have to be *abbreviated*? Circle your answers.

a. It is hard to understand.
b. There are too many corrections.
c. It takes too much time.
d. It is too long.

Day 3 abbreviate • abbreviation

1. How would you complete these sentences? Say them aloud to a partner.

Calendars often abbreviate the _______.

One abbreviation I know is _______.

2. How many words are *abbreviated* in this sentence? Circle your answer.

My address is 123 Palm St., Orlando, FL.

a. one
b. two
c. three
d. four

3. Match each word with its *abbreviation*. Draw lines to show the matches.

a. Tuesday	OH
b. Avenue	Feb.
c. February	Ave.
d. Ohio	Tues.

Day 4 pause

1. How would you complete these sentences? Say them aloud to a partner.

I might take a pause from my homework in order to _______.

When I'm reading, I sometimes pause to _______.

2. In which sentence is the word *pause* used correctly? Circle your answer.

a. The student read to the end of the pause.
b. After a pause to catch her breath, the runner continued.
c. The dog limped because it had a thorn in its pause.
d. The audience greeted the band with a pause.

3. When should you *pause* when you are reading aloud? Circle your answers.

a. at the end of a sentence
b. after a long word
c. at the end of every line
d. at a comma

Day 5 **brief • abbreviate**
abbreviation • pause

Fill in the bubble next to the correct answer.

1. Which of the following could be described as *brief*?

Ⓐ a three-month vacation
Ⓑ a four-hour movie
Ⓒ a one-minute song
Ⓓ a ten-page poem

2. Which word has the same meaning as *abbreviate*?

Ⓕ revise
Ⓖ edit
Ⓗ shorten
Ⓙ relieve

3. Which of the following sentences contains an *abbreviation*?

Ⓐ Dr. Kim is Justin's dentist.
Ⓑ He goes to the dentist in March and September.
Ⓒ Justin's checkup is next Thursday.
Ⓓ Her office is on Maple Avenue.

4. In which sentence could the word *paused* be used to fill in the blank?

Ⓕ The children ______ off the TV and got ready for bed.
Ⓖ Mom ______ to their room to tuck them in and read to them.
Ⓗ After reading a page, Mom ______ and wondered if anyone was still awake.
Ⓙ Two pages later, she ______ the lights and whispered, "Good night."

Writing Write about what you are going to do on Saturday and Sunday. Use *abbreviations* in your writing.

____

____

____

define

DAY 1

(verb) To explain or tell the meaning of a word or phrase.

*We **define** words when we tell what they mean.*

definition

DAY 2

(noun) The meaning of a word or phrase.

*The **definition** of "edit" is "to check for and correct errors in writing."*

definite

DAY 3

(adj.) Known for sure; certain.

*We are waiting for a **definite** answer from Aunt Caitlin about when she is coming to visit.*

definitely

DAY 4

(adv.) Without a doubt.

*Jeremy will **definitely** finish his homework before bedtime.*

Day 1 define

1. How would you complete this sentence? Say it aloud to a partner.

I would define the word "happy" as ________.

2. Which of these phrases *defines* the word "smooth"? Circle your answer.

a. rocky point
b. not rough
c. rough or lumpy
d. a calm sea

3. Which sentence correctly uses the word *define*? Circle your answer.

a. Clare defined her garden with flowers and vegetables.
b. Nina defined "brief" by saying it has the same meaning as "short."
c. Elijah defined his cats Whiskers and Swishy Tail.
d. Emil defined his invitation to the party.

Day 2 definition

1. How would you complete this sentence? Say it aloud to a partner.

Knowing the definitions for words is important when I read because ________.

2. Which of these words has about the same meaning as *definition*? Circle your answer.

a. idea
b. invention
c. meaning
d. feature

3. Match each of these words with its *definition*. Draw lines to show your answers.

a. noticeable	the writer of a story, book, article, or play
b. familiar	to have or own something
c. author	able to be noticed or seen
d. possess	well-known

Day 3 definite

1. How would you complete this sentence? Say it aloud to a partner.

My family has made definite plans to ________.

2. Which of the following things is most likely to be *definite*? Circle your answer.

a. when you will be in school this week
b. your vacation plans for the year 2030
c. where you will go to college
d. who will win a contest

3. In which sentence could the underlined word or words be replaced by the word *definite*? Circle your answer.

a. It can be hard to explain the meaning of some words.
b. Fred is unsure about his plans to go to the beach.
c. The group came up with a very original answer to the problem.
d. Amanda was not able to give a certain answer.

Day 4 definitely

1. How would you complete this sentence? Say it aloud to a partner.

Spinach pizza is definitely ________.

2. In which sentences is the word *definitely* used correctly? Circle your answers.

a. Quentin was definitely about which books he liked.
b. Ella could definitely use some help carrying the heavy box.
c. Everyone decorated his or her mailbox definitely.
d. He had studied hard and was definitely ready for the test.

3. Which two words have about the same meaning as *definitely*? Circle your answers.

a. possibly
b. believably
c. certainly
d. absolutely

Day 5 define • definition definite • definitely

Fill in the bubble next to the correct answer.

1. When you *define a* word, you ________.

Ⓐ learn how to spell it
Ⓑ write it neatly and carefully
Ⓒ tell what it means
Ⓓ say it without pausing

2. Which of these is a *definition* for "differently"?

Ⓕ adjective
Ⓖ four syllables
Ⓗ noun
Ⓙ in a way that is not the same

3. In which sentence could the word *definite* be used to fill in the blank?

Ⓐ We have ________ plans to see a movie this weekend.
Ⓑ The story was very dreamlike and ________.
Ⓒ Because she was nervous, her voice sounded ________.
Ⓓ She was not sure about her ________ answer.

4. The dog *definitely* needs a bath because ________.

Ⓕ he hates getting wet
Ⓖ he has long hair
Ⓗ we bought some new dog shampoo
Ⓙ he was rolling in the mud

Writing Tell about something you will *definitely* do in the next week. Be sure to use the word *definitely* in your writing.

____

____

____

increase

DAY 1

(verb) To make greater or larger.

*We will **increase** our classroom library by adding more books.*

increase

DAY 2

(noun) A greater amount of something.

*The movie theater announced an **increase** in the cost of a ticket.*

decrease

DAY 3

(verb) To make or become less.

*Healthy habits can **decrease** the number of colds you get.*

decrease

DAY 4

(noun) The amount by which something becomes less.

*The flu caused a **decrease** in school attendance.*

Day 1 increase

1. How would you complete this sentence? Say it aloud to a partner.

I want to increase my _______ collection.

2. Which phrase best completes this sentence? Circle your answer.

The school increased its size by _______.

a. painting it white
b. building more rooms
c. planting a garden
d. giving more homework

3. Which sentence correctly uses the word *increase*? Circle your answer.

a. Turning down the radio will increase the noise in your bedroom.
b. The air conditioner will increase the room.
c. Doing your math homework is likely to increase your score on the test.
d. Losing two players increased the size of our team.

Day 2 increase

1. How would you complete this sentence? Say it aloud to a partner.

I would like to ask for an increase in _______.

2. In which of the following would you like an *increase*? Circle your answers.

a. your allowance
b. colds
c. bug bites
d. your free time

3. Which amount shows an *increase* over the amount shown in the first glass? Circle the correct glass.

a.

b.

c.

Day 3 decrease

1. How would you complete this sentence? Say it aloud to a partner.

I want to decrease the _______.

2. Which word has about the same meaning as *decrease*? Circle your answer.

a. choose
b. trick
c. increase
d. reduce

3. Which sentence uses the word *decrease* correctly? Circle your answer.

a. We can decrease the time we spend on this if we work faster.
b. Elliot tried to decrease us by not telling the truth.
c. When people move to our community, it decreases the population.
d. We add more water to the glass to decrease the amount.

Day 4 decrease

1. How would you complete this sentence? Say it aloud to a partner.

I would like to see a decrease in _______ because _______.

2. Which of these could cause a *decrease* in your report card marks? Circle your answer.

a. studying
b. neat writing
c. correct answers
d. not doing your homework

3. In which of these things would a *decrease* be a good thing? Circle your answers.

a. your allowance
b. littering
c. air pollution
d. the number of books you read

Day 5 increase • decrease

Fill in the bubble next to the correct answer.

1. In which sentence is the word *increase* used correctly?

Ⓐ The cool breeze increased the heat.
Ⓑ A traffic jam increased the time it took to get to town.
Ⓒ Space travel increased the distance between the moon and Earth.
Ⓓ Studying increased his chances of failing the test.

2. An *increase* in the population means that ______.

Ⓕ there are more people
Ⓖ there are fewer people
Ⓗ people are taller
Ⓙ people live in many places

3. In which sentence could the word *decrease* be used to fill in the blank?

Ⓐ Reading teaches you new words and will ______ your vocabulary.
Ⓑ Exercise will ______ your level of fitness.
Ⓒ More children in school will ______ the need for teachers.
Ⓓ Since bats eat bugs, bats can ______ the insect population.

4. A *decrease* in rainfall could cause ______.

Ⓕ flooding
Ⓖ some plants to die
Ⓗ the rivers to rise
Ⓙ trees to grow faster

Writing Tell about something you would like to see *decreased.* Be sure to use the word *decrease* in your writing.

____

____

____

form
DAY 1

(noun) Type or kind.

*Reading is Jared's favorite **form** of entertainment.*

form
DAY 2

(verb) To make or create; give shape to.

*How do we **form** a triangle?*

form
DAY 3

(verb) To make up or to organize.

*Let's **form** a group to discuss this.*

format • style
DAY 4

format

(noun) The way in which something is made up or organized.

*The simple **format** of the game makes it easy to play.*

---

style

(noun) The way in which something is written, said, or done.

*The writer's **style** is easy to understand.*

Day 1 form

1. How would you complete this sentence? Say it aloud to a partner.

My favorite form of fun is ________.

2. Which of the following are *forms* of exercise? Circle your answers.

a. playing soccer
b. riding the bus
c. riding a bicycle
d. watching a ballgame

3. Which word best completes this sentence? Circle your answer.

Fables are Navaeh's favorite form of ________.

a. flower
b. animal
c. story
d. music

Day 2 form

1. How would you complete this sentence? Say it aloud to a partner.

I can form clay into a ________.

2. Which word or phrase best completes this sentence? Circle your answer.

Rain can form ________.

a. a sunny sky
b. trees
c. mud puddles
d. warm weather

3. Which sentence correctly uses the word *form?* Circle your answer.

a. The bell forms loud and clear.
b. Marianne will form the cookie dough into heart shapes.
c. Flooding can be the form of too much rain.
d. King Kong forms the monster in our play.

Day 3 form

1. How would you complete this sentence? Say it aloud to a partner.

I think it would be fun to form a _______ club.

2. What would people *form* to do each of these things? Draw lines to show your answers.

a. to get on the bus	form a book club
b. to talk about books	form two teams
c. to play a basketball game	form a car pool
d. to take turns driving	form a line

3. Which sentence does <u>not</u> use the word *form* correctly? Circle your answer.

a. The students formed a circle for their reading group.
b. The gym teacher asked the students to form four teams.
c. Brad formed chocolate and milk to make chocolate milk.
d. Ramon formed a group to pick up the trash.

Day 4 format • style

1. How would you complete these sentences? Say them aloud to a partner.

The test format I like most is _______.

Our principal's speaking style is very _______.

2. Which of these things is part of newspaper's *format*? Circle your answers.

a. the size of the newspaper
b. who reads the newspaper
c. how much the newspaper costs
d. how much space is taken up with pictures

3. Which of these phrases describes an author's writing *style*? Circle your answers.

a. uses white paper
b. makes you laugh out loud
c. drives an old car
d. uses long words

Day 5 form • format • style

Fill in the bubble next to the correct answer.

1. Which of the following can be formed?

Ⓐ a poem
Ⓑ a ruler
Ⓒ a computer
Ⓓ a pencil

2. Which sentence does not use the word *form* correctly?

Ⓕ Jill formed jungle animals from clay.
Ⓖ The students formed a group to write a class newspaper.
Ⓗ The stones formed a bridge across the stream.
Ⓙ The book formed a story about an alligator.

3. Which of the following is not part of the *format* of a book?

Ⓐ the size of the pages
Ⓑ long sentences
Ⓒ the number of pictures
Ⓓ where the words appear on the page

4. Which of the following could have a funny *style*?

Ⓕ a desk
Ⓖ a story
Ⓗ a piece of paper
Ⓙ a potato chip

Writing Describe your favorite *form* of after-school activity. Be sure to use the word *form* in your writing.

____

____

____

conclude

DAY 1

(verb) To bring or come to an end.

*The teacher **concluded** the lesson just as the recess bell rang.*

conclusion

DAY 2

(noun) The end or last part of something.

*At the **conclusion** of the story, the lost dog found its way home.*

conclude

DAY 3

(verb) To decide based on the facts you have.

*Henry looked at the paw print and **concluded** that it had been made by a cat.*

conclusion

DAY 4

(noun) A decision reached using the facts and clues you have.

*We studied the clues and drew a **conclusion** about who had eaten the sandwich.*

Day 1 conclude

1. How would you complete this sentence? Say it aloud to a partner.

I like to conclude a friendly letter with ________.

2. In which sentence can the word *conclude* take the place of "end"? Circle your answer.

a. The coach will end his speech by saying, "Go team!"
b. At the end of the game, we cheered our favorite team.
c. Players and fans celebrated the end of a great season.
d. In the end, having fun is more important than winning.

3. How might each of these things *conclude*? Draw lines to show your answers.

a. a fairy tale	with the sun going down
b. a tic-tac-toe game	with the audience clapping
c. a concert	with one player getting three in a row
d. a day	with "and they lived happily ever after"

Day 2 conclusion

1. How would you complete this sentence? Say it aloud to a partner.

I like story conclusions that are ________.

2. Which of these words means the opposite of *conclusion*? Circle your answer.

a. end
b. decision
c. beginning
d. partnership

3. In which sentence is the word *conclusion* not used correctly? Circle your answer.

a. In conclusion, I believe our school should recycle.
b. At the conclusion of the recital, the dancers took a bow.
c. At the conclusion of the school year, we celebrate with a party.
d. At the conclusion of the school day, the bell rings to begin class.

Day 3 conclude

1. How would you complete this sentence? Say it aloud to a partner.

Walking into my bedroom, someone could conclude that ______.

2. What might you *conclude* from each of the clues at the left? Draw lines to show your answers.

a. cat hair on someone's clothes	It is raining outside.
b. people walking with open umbrellas	Someone is at the door.
c. someone yawns	The person has a cat.
d. the dog runs to the door and barks	The person needs a nap.

3. In which sentence could the underlined words be replaced by *conclude*? Circle your answer.

a. Our national parks take in forests, mountains, and shorelines.
b. After listening to Tia, Ben had to think that she knew a lot about whales.
c. Hurrying caused Brianna to leave out a big part of the story.
d. Nicole and her sister never agree about anything.

Day 4 conclusion

1. How would you complete this sentence? Say it aloud to a partner.

When I smell food cooking at home, I come to the conclusion that ______.

2. Which phrase best completes this sentence? Circle your answer.

When I saw Ian carrying a stack of books, I drew the conclusion that ______.

a. he had lost his dog
b. he had been to the library
c. the bookstore ran out of books
d. he was trying to run faster

3. If you saw a bird with twigs in its beak, what *conclusion* might you draw? Circle your answer.

a. Birds eat spiders.
b. There was a scarecrow nearby.
c. It was summer.
d. The bird was building a nest.

Day 5 conclude • conclusion

Fill in the bubble next to the correct answer.

1. Which of these words does not have about the same meaning as *conclude*?

Ⓐ end
Ⓑ finish
Ⓒ complete
Ⓓ cover

2. Which of these things would most likely happen at the *conclusion* of a play?

Ⓕ The curtain would open.
Ⓖ The actors would bow.
Ⓗ The audience would take their seats.
Ⓙ The play would begin.

3. Which sentence does not use the word *conclude* correctly?

Ⓐ The school day will conclude at 3:00.
Ⓑ Let's conclude this book in our reading list.
Ⓒ The vet combed our dog's coat and concluded that he had fleas.
Ⓓ Looking at the puddles, Jake concluded that it had rained hard last night.

4. Which sentence best describes a *conclusion*?

Ⓕ A conclusion is a guess about what will happen next.
Ⓖ A conclusion is a creative idea about something you want to do.
Ⓗ A conclusion is an idea or decision based on what you know.
Ⓙ A conclusion is new idea that no one else has had.

Writing How would you like to *conclude* this school year? Be sure to use the word *conclude* in your writing.

____

____

____

REVIEW: Weeks 1–8

Daily Academic Vocabulary

brief	definitely	increase	subject
decreased	edited	revisions	unusual

Day 1

Fill in the blanks with words from the word box.

Lemurs are strange, ________________ animals. They look like teddy bears with long bushy tails. One surprise is that lemurs are related to apes and monkeys. They seem so different. Lately there has been an ________________ in interest about lemurs. They have been the ________________ of many books. They are ________________ one of the cutest animals around!

Day 2

Fill in the blanks with words from the word box.

Jason was writing a report on space travel. His teacher read Jason's first draft. She made some ________________ to it as she did. Jason then ________________ his story. His second draft had more information on the space shuttle. But now the report was too long. To keep his report ________________, Jason ________________ the number of pages on early space travel.

REVIEW: Weeks 1–8

Daily Academic Vocabulary

abbreviate	conclude	definite	forms	usual
abbreviation	defined	definition	pause	

Day 3

Fill in the blanks with words from the word box.

Energy is all around us. It comes in many different ________________. Energy is ________________ as "the ability to do work." We might ________________ from this ________________ that lazy people have no energy. But all living things use energy. For example, our bodies use energy to keep us alive. Like machines, our heart and lungs never ________________, even when we are asleep. They use energy to keep us running.

Day 4

Fill in the blanks with words from the word box.

Is "AR" the ________________ for Arizona or Arkansas? If you said Arkansas, you're right! It can be tricky to ________________ state names. The ________________ pattern is to use the first two letters of a state's name. But not all states follow this rule. Arizona is AZ, for example. The only ________________ rule is that for states with two-word names, like New York, use the first letter of each word (NY).

Crack the Code!

Write one of the words from the word box on the lines next to each clue.

abbreviate	conclusion	definitely	format	revise	topic
abbreviation	decrease	definition	increase	revision	unusual
brief	define	edit	pause	style	usual
conclude	definite	form	regular	subject	

1. short in time or length ___ ___ ___ ___ ___ (1 under letter 1, 2 under letter 4)

2. to improve something by making it clearer ___ ___ ___ ___ ___ ___ (3 under letter 1)

3. the shape of something ___ ___ ___ ___ (4 under letter 1, 5 under letter 4)

4. to finish ___ ___ ___ ___ ___ ___ ___ ___ (6 under letter 2, 7 under letter 5, 8 under letter 7)

5. the opposite of "decrease" ___ ___ ___ ___ ___ ___ ___ ___ (9 under letter 2, 10 under letter 3, 11 under letter 7)

6. usual or normal ___ ___ ___ ___ ___ ___ ___ (12 under letter 4, 13 under letter 6)

Now use the numbers under the letters to crack the code. Write the letters on the lines below. The words will complete this sentence.

Madagascar is the only place in the world where ______.

___ ___ ___ ___ ___ ___   ___ ___ ___   ___ ___   ___ ___ ___ ___ ___

7 2 5 12 3 11   10 13 9   1 2   4 6 12 9 8

Words for Weeks 10–17

Week 10

arrange
arrangement
arrangements

Week 11

base
basic
basics
basis

Week 12

oppose
opposite

Week 13

sum
total
summary
summarize

Week 14

model
copy

Week 15

suggest
suggestion
claim

Week 16

event
occur
occurrence

Week 17

general
generalize
generalization
exact
exactly

arrange

DAY 1

(verb) To put into a specific order.

*They will **arrange** the words in alphabetical order.*

arrangement

DAY 2

(noun) The way in which things are placed or grouped.

*The **arrangement** of the desks made it easy to move around the room.*

arrange

DAY 3

(verb) To make plans for or prepare.

*Mr. Benson **arranged** for the class to visit the museum.*

arrangements

DAY 4

(noun) The plans for something.

*The librarian made the **arrangements** for a school book fair.*

Day 1 arrange

1. How would you complete this sentence? Say it aloud to a partner.

I can arrange the clothes in my closet by ________.

2. Which sentences correctly use the word *arrange*? Circle your answers.

a. On the test, we had to arrange the words in alphabetical order.
b. Mieko will arrange the water in the pool.
c. Lionel carefully arranged the candles on the cake.
d. There was a huge arrange of food for the party.

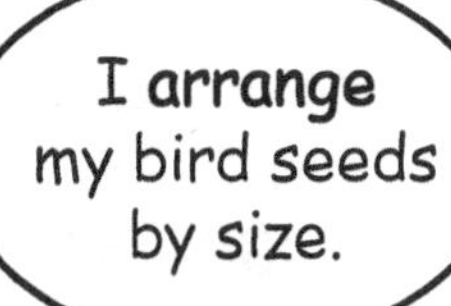

3. Which words or phrases correctly complete this sentence? Circle your answers.

Books in the library are arranged by ________.

a. color
b. subject
c. size
d. author's last name

Day 2 arrangement

1. How would you complete this sentence? Say it aloud to a partner.

I could change the arrangement of my room by ________.

2. Which *arrangement* of shapes is the same as the first *arrangement*? Circle your answer.

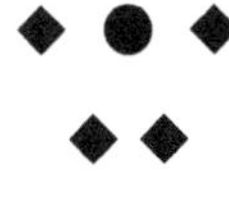

a.

b.

c.

3. Which sentence has the same words but in a different *arrangement*? Circle your answer.

Squirrels are there in the tree.

a. Is the squirrel in the tree?
b. Squirrels live in trees.
c. The tree has squirrels in it.
d. There are squirrels in the tree.

Day 3 arrange

1. How would you complete this sentence? Say it aloud to a partner.

I wish my teacher would arrange for ________.

2. In which sentence is *arranged* not used correctly? Circle your answer.

a. Caitlin arranged to meet Nikia after school.
b. Zoe's parents arranged for the baby sitter to come at 6:00.
c. The children's ages arranged from 6 to 11.
d. The Bartons arranged for someone to mow their lawn.

3. What might you *arrange* if you wanted to do each thing at the left? Draw lines to show your answers.

a. celebrate someone's birthday	arrange a trip to the zoo
b. see lions and tigers	arrange a trip to the vet
c. have shorter hair	arrange a birthday party
d. be sure your pet is healthy	arrange to get a haircut

Day 4 arrangements

1. How would you complete this sentence? Say it aloud to a partner.

I would like to make arrangements to ________ with my friends.

2. In which sentence can *arrangements* not replace the word "plans"? Circle your answer.

a. Marianne's family plans to take a trip.
b. All their travel plans are set.
c. They made plans for a neighbor to feed the cat.
d. They also made plans for the post office to hold their mail.

3. Which of these things require people to make *arrangements?* Circle your answers.

a. carpooling
b. riding a bike
c. reading a book
d. taking a trip on an airplane

Day 5 arrange • arrangement • arrangements

Fill in the bubble next to the correct answer.

1. Which of these things could you *arrange*?

Ⓐ the wall of a building
Ⓑ the trees in a forest
Ⓒ the furniture in a room
Ⓓ the clouds in the sky

2. Which of these words has about the same meaning as *arrangement*?

Ⓕ pattern
Ⓖ reason
Ⓗ sound
Ⓙ apartment

3. Which of these sentences could you complete with the word *arrange*?

Ⓐ We will ________ the bus at the corner.
Ⓑ We will ________ for a bus to take us there.
Ⓒ We will ________ that the bus is here.
Ⓓ We will ________ by bus at 4:15.

4. In which sentence could the underlined word(s) be replaced by *arrangements*?

Ⓕ The school fair was the biggest <u>event</u> of the year.
Ⓖ The third grade was in charge of <u>making decorations</u> for the gym.
Ⓗ The fourth grade was in charge of the <u>entertainment</u>.
Ⓙ The parents' group made <u>plans</u> to have games and prizes.

Writing What would you like to *arrange* to do this weekend? Explain your ideas. Be sure to use the word *arrange* in your writing.

____

____

____

base DAY 1

(noun) The lowest part of something or the part something stands on.

*Moss grew at the **base** of the tree.*

base DAY 2

(verb) To use as a starting point for something else.

*She will **base** her story on an actual event.*

basic • basics DAY 3

basic

(adj.) Forming the main part of something.

*Jayden explained the **basic** idea of the game.*

---

basics

(noun) The most important skills or facts to know.

*Ruby has mastered the **basics** of horseback riding.*

basis DAY 4

(noun) The reasons or ideas behind something.

*Kelly's idea became the **basis** for the whole plan.*

Day 1 base

1. How would you complete this sentence? Say it aloud to a partner.

Something in our classroom that has a base is ________.

2. Which one is the *base* of the statue? Circle the letter.

3. Which phrase best completes this sentence? Circle your answer.

The children ________ around the base of the tree.

a. looked up at the bird's nest
b. climbed on the branches
c. raked the fallen leaves
d. saw birds fly

Day 2 base

1. How would you complete this sentence? Say it aloud to a partner.

I have seen a movie that was based on a ________.

2. Match the book titles to what they are *based* on. Draw lines to show your answers.

a. The Big Plant	"The Frog Prince"
b. Emily and the Enchanted Frog	the author's own life
c. When I Was Young in the Mountains	an African folk tale
d. How Lion Became King of the Animals	"Jack and the Beanstalk"

3. What would not happen in a movie *based* on real life? Circle your answers.

a. Bicycles would fly.
b. It would take place in Kansas.
c. It would be about the past.
d. A scarecrow would come to life.

Day 3 basic • basics

1. How would you complete these sentences? Say them aloud to a partner.

The basic ingredients of my favorite snack are ________.

The basics of riding a bicycle are ________.

2. Which of these is <u>not</u> a *basic* skill you learn in school? Circle your answer.

a. number facts
b. letters and sounds
c. spelling words
d. kite flying

3. Think of a game or sport you know. List the *basics* for playing it.

Topic: soccer
a. dribbling
b. passing
c. receiving

Game or Sport: ____________________

a. ____________________

b. ____________________

c. ____________________

Day 4 basis

1. How would you complete this sentence? Say it aloud to a partner.

The basis of the story I have written is ________.

2. Which of these words does <u>not</u> have about the same meaning as *basis*? Circle your answer.

a. starting point
b. cause
c. basement
d. reason

3. Which sentence could you complete with *basis*? Circle your answer.

a. We can store the wood in the ________.
b. Grandpa taught Xavier the ________ skills of fishing.
c. Amanda's suggestion was the ________ of our group's report.
d. Flowers were planted at the ________ of the flagpole.

Day 5 base • basic • basics • basis

Fill in the bubble next to the correct answer.

1. Which phrase does not tell the meaning of *base*?

Ⓐ the lowest part
Ⓑ the bottom
Ⓒ what something stands on
Ⓓ under the ground

2. Which of the following would a writer be most likely to *base* a story on?

Ⓕ a math problem
Ⓖ a funny thing that happened
Ⓗ a writing desk
Ⓙ a piece of paper

3. Which of the following is not a *basic* skill needed to do crossword puzzles?

Ⓐ knowledge of words
Ⓑ knowledge of word meanings
Ⓒ ability to subtract
Ⓓ ability to spell words correctly

4. Which of the following would probably not be a *basis* for a school project?

Ⓕ wanting to learn about sharks
Ⓖ preparing for the field trip to a museum
Ⓗ talking on the phone
Ⓙ discovering a fossil

Writing Tell about something you would like to *base* a story on. Be sure to use the word *base* in your writing.

____

____

____

oppose
DAY 1

(verb) To be against something.

I'm sure the principal will ***oppose*** *our idea to have a longer recess.*

opposite
DAY 2

(noun) Something or someone that is completely different from another.

Hot is the ***opposite*** *of cold.*

(adj.) As different as possible.

They had ***opposite*** *opinions of the book.*

opposite
DAY 3

(adj.) Facing away or moving the other way.

The library and the office are in ***opposite*** *directions from our room.*

opposite
DAY 4

(adj.) Located directly across; on the other end or side.

We sat on ***opposite*** *ends of the park bench.*

Day 1 oppose

1. How would you complete this sentence? Say it aloud to a partner.

My parents are opposed to me ______.

2. Think about the people listed at the left. What would each group *oppose*? Draw lines to show your answers.

a. animal lovers	cutting down forests
b. people who love trees	litter
c. people who clean up parks and beaches	the library closing
d. people who love to read	being mean to animals

3. Which of these things are you *opposed* to? Circle your answers.

a. longer school days
b. no summer vacation
c. extra homework
d. staying up past your bedtime

Day 2 opposite

1. How would you complete these sentences? Say them aloud to a partner.

______ and ______ are opposites.

My friend and I have opposite opinions about ______.

2. For each word, write a word that means the *opposite*.

a. happy ______________
b. remember ______________
c. easy ______________
d. multiply ______________

3. Which two objects have *opposite* purposes? Circle your answer.

a. a cup and a glass
b. a radio and a CD player
c. a pencil and an eraser
d. a coat and a jacket

Day 3 opposite

1. How would you complete this sentence? Say it aloud to a partner.

From our classroom, _______ and _______ are in opposite directions.

2. Which arrows are pointing in *opposite* directions? Circle your answers.

a.

b.

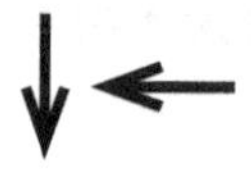
c.

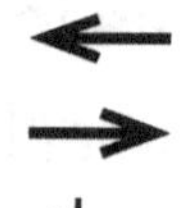
d.

3. Which sentence describes people who are going in *opposite* directions? Circle your answer.

a. Amelia and Tara jogged side by side.

b. Brandon's little brother tagged along behind him.

c. Eliot turned right at the corner, and Colin went left.

d. Ellen walked so fast that Henry had a hard time keeping up.

Day 4 opposite

1. How would you complete this sentence? Say it aloud to a partner.

My home is on the opposite side of the street from _______.

2. Complete each sentence with the phrase that makes sense. Draw lines to show your answers.

a. Anna and Tad walked on opposite	City Hall.
b. The library is on the opposite corner from	side of the room.
c. Tia waved to Gus from the opposite	ends of the table.
d. The king and queen sat at opposite	sides of the street.

3. Which sentence correctly uses the word *opposite*? Circle your answer.

a. The riverbank runs opposite to the river.

b. The two hotels are on opposite ends of the park.

c. The people are opposite to higher gas prices.

d. Gigi's parents opposite her from seeing scary movies.

Day 5 oppose • opposite

Fill in the bubble next to the correct answer.

1. Which sentence uses the word *oppose* correctly?

Ⓐ Peter sat at the table opposed to door.
Ⓑ The word "private" is opposed to "public."
Ⓒ People are opposed to tearing down the old hotel.
Ⓓ The lion statues are on opposed sides of the door.

2. Which word is the *opposite* of "shout"?

Ⓕ yell
Ⓖ whisper
Ⓗ scream
Ⓙ shouted

3. If two people walk in *opposite* directions, ________.

Ⓐ one walks fast and the other walks slow
Ⓑ one follows the other
Ⓒ one walks forward and the other walks behind
Ⓓ one goes left and the other goes right

4. If Jaime and Xander live in *opposite* parts of town, which sentence might be true?

Ⓕ Jaime and Xander both live close to the school.
Ⓖ Jaime lives north of town, and Xander lives east of town.
Ⓗ Jaime and Xander ride the bus to school.
Ⓙ Jaime lives in the north of town, and Xander lives in the south of town.

Writing What is something you are *opposed* to? Explain why you *oppose* it. Be sure to use the word *oppose* in your writing.

____

____

____

sum
DAY 1

(noun) A number that you get by adding two or more numbers.

*The **sum** of 5 and 8 is 13.*

total
DAY 2

(noun) The whole amount.

*A **total** of 50 states are in the United States.*

(adj.) Making up the whole amount.

*The **total** population of the world is 6.5 billion.*

total
DAY 3

(verb) To find the sum of numbers.

***Total** the number correct before turning in your quiz.*

summary • summarize
DAY 4

summary

(noun) A short statement giving the main points of something that has been written or spoken.

*Leah gave a **summary** of what the principal said in her speech.*

---

summarize

(verb) To give the main points of something that has been written or spoken.

*All students **summarized** their book reports for the class.*

Day 1 sum

1. How would you complete this sentence? Say it aloud to a partner.

The sum of ________ and ________ is ________.

2. Which number in this number sentence is the *sum?* Circle your answer.

12 + 31 + 17 = 60

a. 17 c. 12
b. 60 d. 31

3. In which sentence could you use *sum* to fill in the blank? Circle your answer.

a. Gabriela divided 24 by 8 to get the ________ of 3.
b. Justin subtracted 57 from 83 to get the ________ of 26.
c. Chloe multiplied 7 by 9 to get the ________ of 63.
d. Rashid added 10, 81, and 37 to get the ________ of 128.

Day 2 total

1. How would you complete these sentences? Say them aloud to a partner.

So far this week, I have read a total of ________.

I would like to know the total number of people who ________.

2. Which number is the *total* of these shapes? Circle your answer.

a. 4 c. 2
b. 3 d. 1

3. The *total population* of the class is 17 students. Which phrase has about the same meaning as the underlined words? Circle your answer.

a. the sum of all the girls in the class
b. the number of students in the school
c. the sum of all the students in the class
d. the number of students living on Earth

Day 3 total

1. How would you complete this sentence? Say it aloud to a partner.

I can total the number of ______ in my classroom.

2. Which problem requires that you *total*? Circle your answer.

a. 8 – 3 c. 7 – 4
b. 2 × 5 d. 3 + 5

3. In which sentence can *total* replace the word "add"? Circle your answer.

a. Ben wanted to add toppings to the pizza.
b. Mom reminded him it would add to the cost.
c. The waiter will add all the charges.
d. Mom will add a tip to the final bill.

Day 4 summary • summarize

1. How would you complete these sentences? Say them aloud to a partner.

I could give a summary of ______.

I can summarize my weekend by ______.

2. Which phrase best completes this sentence? Circle your answer.

Mateo will summarize the book ______.

a. before reading it
b. in his book report
c. before checking it out of the library
d. by reading it on vacation

3. Which of the following things is not true about a *summary*? Circle your answer.

a. It is short.
b. It tells the main ideas.
c. It tells every detail.
d. It includes only what is important.

Day 5 sum • total • summary • summarize

Fill in the bubble next to the correct answer.

1. Which problem has an answer that is a *sum?*

Ⓐ 12 – 7 = ____

Ⓑ 3 × 4 = ____

Ⓒ 8 + 10 = ____

Ⓓ 15 – 2 = ____

2. In which sentence could *sum* take the place of *total?*

Ⓕ Karin wanted to know the total number of pets in her class.

Ⓖ She found out the total dog population.

Ⓗ She would total that with the number of cats, fish, and gerbils.

Ⓙ The total would be all her classmates' pets.

3. When you *total* a set of something you ________.

Ⓐ order them from least to greatest

Ⓑ add them all together

Ⓒ find the average

Ⓓ group the odd and even numbers

4. Which of these things would you probably <u>not</u> *summarize?*

Ⓕ a book

Ⓖ pictures

Ⓗ a speech

Ⓙ a story

Writing *Summarize* your favorite memory. Describe what happened. Be sure to use the word *summary* or *summarize* in your writing.

____

____

____

model
DAY 1

(noun) A small version of something.
*We built a **model** of a volcano in science class.*

(verb) To use something as the plan or idea for something else.
*Lucy **modeled** her cat painting after her pet Fluffy.*

model
DAY 2

(adj.) Ideal or perfect.
*Tomás is a **model** citizen because he is nice to people, helps out in the community, and obeys the law.*

copy
DAY 3

(noun) Something that looks or sounds exactly like another thing.
*The museum built the dinosaur using **copies** of the original bones.*

(noun) One of a number of things that were printed at the same time.
*Angel brought a **copy** of his favorite book to class.*

copy
DAY 4

(verb) To write down the same way.
*After the teacher writes the question on the board, we **copy** it onto our papers.*

(verb) To do the same as somebody or something else.
*The monkeys in the zoo **copied** my funny faces.*

Day 1 model

1. How would you complete these sentences? Say them aloud to a partner.

I would like to make a model of a ________.

I could model a sand castle after ________.

2. Which of the following are *models* of something larger? Circle your answers.

a. a baby doll
b. a toy railroad set
c. a garbage truck
d. a library

3. Which sentence correctly uses the word *model*? Circle your answer.

a. They modeled the tree after a seed.
b. Some people model their cars after the color red.
c. Trinity modeled her painting after one she had seen in a book.
d. Alyssa modeled her hair after curls.

Day 2 model

1. How would you complete this sentence? Say it aloud to a partner.

I think a ________ is a model pet because ________.

2. Which word or words might describe a *model* teacher? Circle your answers.

a. fair
b. forgiving
c. forgetful
d. hard to understand

3. Think of a *model* person and list three words that describe him or her.

Person: nurse
a. calm
b. friendly
c. caring

Person: ________________

a. ________________

b. ________________

c. ________________

Day 3 copy

1. How would you complete these sentences? Say them aloud to a partner.

Once in the classroom, I made a copy of ________.

I can find a copy of the ________ in the library.

2. Which shape is a *copy* of the first shape? Circle your answer.

a. b. c.

3. Which phrase best completes this sentence? Circle your answer.

Isabella brought a copy of ________ to school.

a. her dog
b. the ball
c. the newspaper
d. her new hat

Day 4 copy

1. How would you complete these sentences? Say them aloud to a partner.

My teacher asked us to copy ________.

I think it's fun to copy the sounds made by a ________.

2. Which phrase best completes this sentence? Circle your answer.

I like to copy the ________.

a. tree growing in the yard
b. tall building in the city
c. blue car driving on the road
d. barking sounds made by the dog

3. Which of the following might you *copy* from the board onto a piece of paper? Circle your answers.

a. a sentence
b. a poem
c. a marker
d. an eraser

Day 5 model • copy

Fill in the bubble next to the correct answer.

1. Which sentence uses the word *model* correctly?

Ⓐ I was asked to model the letter and send it to Aaron.
Ⓑ Joshua's pet cat Lucy is a model of a lion.
Ⓒ There was a model of the spaceship in the museum.
Ⓓ Each student had a model of the book.

2. An important quality of a *model* singer is ________.

Ⓕ being small
Ⓖ being able to sing in tune
Ⓗ having red hair
Ⓙ knowing other singers

3. In which sentence could the word *copy* be used to fill in the blank?

Ⓐ Every student received a ________ of the book.
Ⓑ The Ice King 2.0 is the latest ________ of refrigerator.
Ⓒ A globe is a ________ of the Earth.
Ⓓ A ________ student always turns in her homework.

4. In which sentence could the underlined words be replaced by the word *copy*?

Ⓕ The toy airplane was a <u>small version</u> of the big jet.
Ⓖ Amy was the <u>ideal</u> helper at home.
Ⓗ Emma used her dream as the <u>idea</u> for a new story.
Ⓙ We tried to <u>write down</u> the words exactly as they were printed.

Writing Describe something that you have *copied* or have seen a *copy* of. Be sure to use the word *copy* in your writing.

____

____

____

suggest • suggestion

DAY 1

suggest

(verb) To offer something as an idea.

*I **suggest** that we watch a movie.*

---

suggestion

(noun) An offered idea or thought.

*It was Darin's **suggestion** to go hiking.*

suggest

DAY 2

(verb) To give a hint of something else or offer clues.

*Dark clouds **suggest** that it might rain.*

claim

DAY 3

(verb) To say that something is true.

*Amanda **claims** that her dog had eleven puppies.*

claim

DAY 4

(verb) To get something or to say that something is yours.

*The best speller will **claim** first place at the spelling bee.*

Day 1 suggest • suggestion

1. How would you complete these sentences? Say them aloud to a partner.

My parents will often suggest ______.

I try to follow my teacher's suggestion to ______.

2. Which phrase best completes this sentence? Circle your answer.

If you suggest hamburgers for dinner, you ______.

a. help make them
b. order them
c. say you would like them
d. eat two of them

3. Which of these statements is a *suggestion*? Circle your answer.

a. Come over here right now!
b. Where are we going?
c. Will's mom took us to the video store.
d. You should see The Wizard of Oz.

Day 2 suggest

1. How would you complete this sentence? Say it aloud to a partner.

My school desk suggests that I ______.

2. In which sentence could *suggest* take the place of the underlined words? Circle your answer.

a. Dishes in the sink are a clue that they need to be washed.
b. Clean hands and enough sleep are ways to prevent colds.
c. Apples and grapes are examples of healthy snacks.
d. Two Dr. Seuss books are on my list of books to read.

3. Each action on the left *suggests* a statement on the right. Draw lines to show the matches.

a. lots of scratching	The neighbors are going on a trip.
b. putting suitcases in the car	The woman has more than one cat.
c. buying a big bag of cat food	The person is in a hurry.
d. walking fast	The dog has fleas.

Day 3 claim

1. How would you complete this sentence? Say it aloud to a partner.

My friend claims that ________.

2. Which of the following would a scientist <u>not</u> *claim?* Circle your answers.

a. Pollution is bad for the Earth.
b. Sitting too close to the TV could hurt your eyes.
c. Exercise is not good for you.
d. Candy is a healthy food.

3. What might someone who loves math *claim?* Circle your answer.

a. I hate math.
b. I'm a good math student.
c. Math is boring.
d. I'd rather do anything than study math.

Day 4 claim

1. How would you complete this sentence? Say it aloud to a partner.

One thing I claim credit for at home is ________.

2. Which of the following would someone <u>not</u> want to *claim?* Circle your answer.

a. blame for doing something bad
b. credit for doing something good
c. first prize in a contest
d. a reward for finding a lost pet

3. Which phrase best completes this sentence? Circle your answer.

Because no one claimed the coat, ________.

a. it was black
b. it fell on the floor
c. it went in the lost and found box
d. it was everyone's favorite

Day 5 suggest • suggestion • claim

Fill in the bubble next to the correct answer.

1. Which sentence could you complete with the word *suggest?*

Ⓐ Our teacher expects us to ________ our homework.
Ⓑ Our teacher asked us to ________ new books to read.
Ⓒ Our teacher asked us to ________ our parents' permission.
Ⓓ Our teacher reminded us to ________ our names on our work.

2. Which sentence uses the word *suggestion* correctly?

Ⓕ Marcus drew a suggestion of the stars.
Ⓖ Bibi didn't keep her suggestion to help.
Ⓗ It was Sam's suggestion to do the project on stars.
Ⓙ A scary story might suggestion a small child.

3. Gray skies and people carrying umbrellas *suggest* that it is ________.

Ⓐ time to play outside
Ⓑ time go sledding
Ⓒ hot and sunny
Ⓓ raining

4. In which sentence is the word *claim* <u>not</u> used correctly?

Ⓕ Melissa claims she is an excellent skater.
Ⓖ Lionel claimed credit for winning the game.
Ⓗ Josh claimed to the teacher yesterday.
Ⓙ Avery claimed the idea was his.

Writing Where would you like to go for your next class field trip? Tell where you would like to go and why. Use the word *suggest* or *suggestion* in your writing.

____

____

____

event
DAY 1

(noun) Something that happens, especially something interesting or important.

*Field Day is a big **event** at our school.*

occur
DAY 2

(verb) To take place or happen.

*Thunderstorms often **occur** during the summer.*

occur
DAY 3

(verb) To come to mind.

*Ideas often **occur** to me while I'm reading.*

occurrence
DAY 4

(noun) Something that takes place.

*Snow is a common winter **occurrence** in Switzerland.*

Day 1 event

1. How would you complete this sentence? Say it aloud to a partner.

So far, the biggest event for me this year was ________.

2. Which of these things would you consider an *event*? Circle your answers.

a. a parade
b. a discussion in class
c. a band concert
d. playing tag on the playground

3. List three *events* that happen in your community.

a. ______________________________

b. ______________________________

c. ______________________________

Day 2 occur

1. How would you complete this sentence? Say it aloud to a partner.

________ occurs every week.

2. In which sentence can *occur* not take the place of the underlined word or words? Circle your answer.

a. The meeting will take place at 4:00 p.m.
b. Recess breaks happen at the same time every day.
c. The clerk asked everyone to take a place in line.
d. How did these mistakes come about?

3. List three things that you know will *occur* in the next two days.

a. ______________________________

b. ______________________________

c. ______________________________

Day 3 occur

1. How would you complete this sentence? Say it aloud to a partner.

When I woke up today, it occurred to me that ________.

2. Which sentence can you complete with the word *occur*? Circle your answer.

a. Frieda ________ an idea for a project.
b. Ideas often ________ to her on a walk.
c. On the walk home, she ________ an idea.
d. Now she must ________ it to her teammates.

3. Which of these things might suddenly *occur* to you? Circle your answers.

a. a book report
b. the idea for a story
c. a map of the world
d. what something reminds you of

Day 4 occurrence

1. How would you complete this sentence? Say it aloud to a partner.

________ is a common occurrence in my home.

2. Which phrase best completes this sentence? Circle your answer.

Celebrations are a regular occurrence ________.

a. on Mondays
b. for one person
c. on holidays
d. for people who hate noise

3. Which word means about the same thing as *occurrence*? Circle your answer.

a. exit
b. disagreement
c. event
d. memory

Day 5 event • occur • occurrence

Fill in the bubble next to the correct answer.

1. Which sentence could you not complete with the word *event*?

Ⓐ The school play is a big ________ in the school year.

Ⓑ A birthday party is a special ________.

Ⓒ At the end of the game, the scores were ________.

Ⓓ The county fair was the biggest ________ of the summer.

2. The longest day of the year always *occurs* ________.

Ⓕ in winter

Ⓖ in summer

Ⓗ when it's night

Ⓙ on Saturday

3. Which sentence could you complete with the word *occurred*?

Ⓐ The idea ________ to her to start a club.

Ⓑ Liang ________ playing soccer every day.

Ⓒ Brianna ________ her idea with the rest of the class.

Ⓓ The thought of swimming in the river ________ him.

4. In which sentence could the word *event* be replaced by *occurrence*?

Ⓕ The parade is a major event in our town.

Ⓖ They are planning a special event to celebrate the day.

Ⓗ A full moon is a regular event.

Ⓙ A visit from Grandma was a big event at Hoon's house.

Writing Tell about an *event* that you are looking forward to. Be sure to use the word *event* in your writing.

____

____

____

general DAY 1

(adj.) Having to do with everybody or everything.

*There was **general** interest in going to the water park.*

general • generalize DAY 2

general

(adj.) Having to do with only the main parts or ideas.

*Wendy gave us a **general** idea of what we had to do for the party.*

generalize

(verb) To form a rule from a small number of specific examples.

*The teacher can **generalize** that her students know addition from their high test scores.*

generalization DAY 3

(noun) A statement or idea that is general, or not specific.

*Saying that dogs like riding in cars is a **generalization**.*

exact • exactly DAY 4

exact

(adj.) Correct and right in every way.

*We know the **exact** number of people in the play.*

exactly

(adv.) In the correct or right way.

*Franco's answer was **exactly** right.*

Day 1 general

1. How would you complete this sentence? Say it aloud to a partner.

Our class showed general agreement about ________.

2. Which of the following would show *general* surprise? Circle your answer.

a. Someone fainted.

b. Everyone's mouths dropped open.

c. A few people clapped their hands.

d. Several people laughed.

3. In which sentence is the word *general* <u>not</u> used correctly? Circle your answer.

a. One student's grade proves general improvement for the whole class.

b. Class art supplies are for general use.

c. There was general support for planting more trees.

d. The new cafeteria menu was met with general approval.

Day 2 general • generalize

1. How would you complete these sentences? Say them aloud to a partner.

I have only a general idea about ________.

From my homework scores, I can generalize that ________.

2. Which of these parts of a book can give you a *general* idea of what a book is about? Circle your answers.

a. title of the book

b. cover of the book

c. the author's name

d. color of the cover

3. What can you *generalize* about schools? Circle your answer.

a. Yours is the best.

b. They help you learn.

c. Some have art programs.

d. You have to go to school.

Day 3 generalization

1. How would you complete this sentence? Say it aloud to a partner.

It is a generalization to say that all dogs ________.

2. Which of these sentences is a *generalization*? Circle your answer.

a. Jason read a book about lizards.
b. A gecko is a kind of lizard.
c. All lizards eat insects.
d. Akiko has a pet lizard.

3. Which of these statements is true about a *generalization*? Circle your answers.

a. It makes a general statement.
b. It talks about just one person or thing.
c. It tells all the facts.
d. It may not be true for everyone or everything.

Day 4 exact • exactly

1. How would you complete these sentences? Say them aloud to a partner.

My exact address is ________.

I was exactly right when I ________.

2. Which pattern is an *exact* copy of the pattern in the box? Circle your answer.

Box	a.	b.	c.
□ ○ △ □	□ ○ □ △	□ ○ ▽ □	□ ○ △ □

3. Which sentence correctly uses the word *exactly*? Circle your answer.

a. Vito guessed that path was exactly 7 miles long.
b. Maura knew that she had exactly $2.73 in her pocket.
c. Bianca gave us a general idea of exactly what she wanted.
d. Because the sun was high in the sky, Tim figured it was exactly noon.

Day 5 general • generalize • generalization exact • exactly

Fill in the bubble next to the correct answer.

1. When there is a *general* understanding, ______.

Ⓐ most people think the same thing
Ⓑ some people tell others how they feel
Ⓒ a few people might have the same opinion
Ⓓ no one knows very much

2. If someone gets the *general* idea, she ______.

Ⓕ understands all the facts completely
Ⓖ finds out what everyone else knows
Ⓗ gets the basic idea
Ⓙ agrees with everybody else

3. Which sentence is a *generalization*?

Ⓐ Some teachers are nice.
Ⓑ My teacher is funny.
Ⓒ All teachers are strict.
Ⓓ Many teachers like to travel.

4. In which sentence could the word *exactly* be used to fill in the blank?

Ⓕ The plane arrived at ______ 8:24 p.m.
Ⓖ When fully grown, he thinks this puppy will weigh ______ 60 pounds.
Ⓗ He couldn't see the clock, but he thought it was ______ 3 o'clock.
Ⓙ He guessed that the drive would take ______ half an hour.

Writing What is something that people *generalize* about kids that you think is wrong? Why do you think it is wrong? Be sure to use the word *generalize* in your writing.

____

____

____

REVIEW: Weeks 10–17

Daily Academic Vocabulary

arrangement	basics	occur	sum
basic	exactly	suggest	total

Day 1

Fill in the blanks with words from the word box.

You can use clouds to do ________________ weather forecasting. The shape and ______________________, or grouping, of clouds can help you predict what the weather will be. Clouds that look like rows of fuzzy bubbles ________________ that cold weather is coming. If it is warm and humid, big clouds with flat tops tell you that a thunderstorm may ________________.

Day 2

Fill in the blanks with words from the word box.

Adding is one of the ________________ of math. When you add, you ________________ numbers to find the ________________. When you add, you should always check your answer to be sure it is ________________ right. You can use a calculator to check your answers. Answers can't be "almost right" when you add.

REVIEW: Weeks 10–17

Daily Academic Vocabulary

arrange	generalization	occurrence	summarize	copies
modeled	opposite	summary	events	

Day 3

Fill in the blanks with words from the word box.

When you ________________ a story, you tell the main ideas of the story. You tell who the characters are. You tell what the problem is. Then you retell the important ________________. You should describe each ________________ in the order in which it happened. Your ________________ should give someone who hasn't read the story a good idea of what happens and why.

Day 4

Fill in the blanks with words from the word box.

Ms. Pearson's class decided to ________________ the furniture to make a Reading Corner. They ________________ the space after a corner in the public library. They stocked the bookshelves with their favorite books and ________________ of children's magazines. They placed three beanbag chairs ________________ the bookshelves. We can make a ________________ that everyone loves the Reading Corner!

Day 5

Crossword Challenge

For each clue, write one of the words from the word box to complete the puzzle.

arrangements	basis	exact	oppose
base	claim	general	suggestion

Across

1. the ideas behind something
5. an idea or thought offered to help
8. to be against something

Down

2. the plan for something
3. to say that something is yours
4. bottom
6. having to do with everyone
7. correct in every way

Words for Weeks 19–26

Week 19
consider
decide
decision

Week 20
attempt
fail
failure

Week 21
question
inquire
inquiry

Week 22
contain
consist
include

Week 23
produce
productive
product

Week 24
cause
effect
effective

Week 25
handle
control

Week 26
recall
recount
memorize
recite

consider
DAY 1

(verb) To think about something carefully.

*The class will **consider** many topics before choosing one to write on.*

consider
DAY 2

(verb) To believe to be true.

*Many people **consider** our school to be the best in the city.*

decide
DAY 3

(verb) To make up your mind about something.

*Our teacher **decides** which books we will read for book reports.*

decision
DAY 4

(noun) A final choice or judgment.

*Our group discussed the choices before making a **decision**.*

Day 1 consider

1. How would you complete this sentence? Say it aloud to a partner.

When I choose a book to read, I consider ______.

2. Which of these things must you *consider* when you do a word problem in math? Circle your answers.

a. what you need to find out
b. if all the words are spelled right
c. how many words are in the problem
d. if you need to add, subtract, multiply, or divide

3. Which phrase best completes this sentence? Circle your answer.

When you consider your choices, you ______.

a. can't decide what to do
b. think hard before deciding
c. do the first thing that comes to mind
d. decide not to do anything

Day 2 consider

1. How would you complete this sentence? Say it aloud to a partner.

I consider math to be ______.

2. Which sentence can you complete with *consider*? Circle your answer.

a. Audra and Kim ______ math more than science.
b. Dipak would ______ read than do anything else.
c. Teachers always ______ Husna to write more.
d. What do you ______ to be your best subject in school?

3. Tell what you *consider* to be each of the following. Write your answers on the lines.

a. the best book ____________________

b. the best movie ____________________

c. the best sport ____________________

Day 3 decide

1. How would you complete this sentence? Say it aloud to a partner.

To decide what to do after school, I will ________.

2. Which of these things can you *decide* for yourself? Circle your answers.

a. what you will be taught today
b. whether you will have homework
c. what ice-cream flavor is your favorite
d. what is in your book report

3. Which sentence does not use the word *decide* correctly? Circle your answer.

a. The book group will decide which book to read next.
b. The judges will decide who the winner is.
c. They flipped a coin to decide which movie to see.
d. Teachers decide students to make an effort.

Day 4 decision

1. How would you complete this sentence? Say it aloud to a partner.

When I have to make a decision, I ________.

2. Which of the following are ways to make a *decision*? Circle your answers.

a. voting
b. arguing
c. choosing
d. not thinking about it

3. Which one does not require making *decisions*? Circle your answer.

a. ordering a pizza
b. following directions
c. painting a picture
d. getting dressed for school

Wearing this hat was a good **decision**!

Day 5 consider • decide • decision

Fill in the bubble next to the correct answer.

1. If you *consider* a problem, it means that you ________.

Ⓐ think hard about it

Ⓑ try to avoid it

Ⓒ make things hard for others

Ⓓ use math to figure it out

2. If you *consider* something to be a problem, it means that you ________.

Ⓕ do it in math

Ⓖ make up your mind about it

Ⓗ think it's troublesome or hard

Ⓙ made it up yourself

3. Which sentence can you complete with the word *decide*?

Ⓐ Kirsten will ________ Soo Ha to be her partner.

Ⓑ They will ________ a social studies project.

Ⓒ First they need to ________ on a topic to study.

Ⓓ Then they will read to ________ about their topic.

4. Which of the following is a *decision* that you can make?

Ⓕ when the sun comes up

Ⓖ whether or not it rains

Ⓗ what you do in your free time

Ⓙ when school is over for the day

Writing What is the hardest *decision* you have ever made? Be sure to use one of this week's words in your writing.

____

____

____

attempt
DAY 1

(verb) To try to do something.

*Colin will **attempt** to stand on his head.*

attempt
DAY 2

(noun) An effort to try to do something.

*Anna's first **attempt** to hit the ball was a success!*

fail
DAY 3

(verb) To try to do something and not be able to do it.

*You may **fail** the first time, but don't give up.*

failure
DAY 4

(noun) Someone or something that is not successful.

*Monty's first attempt to fly a kite was a **failure**.*

Day 1 attempt

1. How would you complete this sentence? Say it aloud to a partner.

When I attempt something new, I ________.

2. What might each one *attempt* to do? Draw lines to show your answers.

a. A good skater might attempt	to win a race.
b. Someone who likes to write might attempt	to swim the length of the pool.
c. A good swimmer might attempt	to write a book.
d. A fast runner might attempt	to skate backward.

3. List three things you would like to *attempt*.

a. ____

b. ____

c. ____

Day 2 attempt

1. How would you complete this sentence? Say it aloud to a partner.

My first attempt to ________ turned out ________.

2. In which sentence could *attempt* <u>not</u> replace the underlined word? Circle your answer.

a. After just one <u>try</u>, Carlo broke the piñata.
b. Gillian made a final <u>effort</u> to help her team win.
c. I took the <u>chance</u> to catch up on my homework.
d. It was our first <u>shot</u> at making ice cream.

3. Which of these things are examples of *attempts*? Circle your answers.

a. a change of plans
b. a swing at the ball
c. a splinter in your finger
d. a guess at the right answer

Day 3 fail

1. How would you complete this sentence? Say it aloud to a partner.

I think I might fail if I tried to ______.

2. Which phrase best completes this sentence? Circle your answer.

Jason failed to finish his paper because ______.

a. he wasn't neat
b. he misspelled some words
c. he ran out of time
d. he wrote it too quickly

3. Complete each sentence by writing the word *fail.*

I don't plan on **failing** the spelling test!

a. If you lose, you ______ to win.

b. If you forget, you ______ to remember.

c. If you miss something, you ______ to notice it.

Day 4 failure

1. How would you complete this sentence? Say it aloud to a partner.

It was a failure the first time I attempted to ______.

2. Which of the following are examples of *failure?* Circle your answers.

a. a chair that breaks
b. a TV that turns on
c. a pie that tastes good
d. a plant that does not grow

3. Tell about a time when you failed. What did you learn from your *failure?*

______

______

______

Day 5 attempt • fail • failure

Fill in the bubble next to the correct answer.

1. If you *attempt* to win a race, you ________.

Ⓐ prove you can run faster than anyone
Ⓑ watch to see who will win
Ⓒ know you will win
Ⓓ try to be the first one to finish

2. Which sentence could you complete with the word *attempt*?

Ⓕ Zoe's report card was an ________ to her parents.
Ⓖ This is Matt's latest ________ to invent a better pencil.
Ⓗ Ellen used the party as the ________ for a new story.
Ⓙ Eddie blamed his ________ on being tired.

3. Which of these things could cause a picnic to *fail*?

Ⓐ happy people
Ⓑ good food
Ⓒ heavy rain
Ⓓ a gentle breeze

4. If someone is a *failure* at hide and seek, they probably ________.

Ⓕ hide too well
Ⓖ find their friends too fast
Ⓗ count too fast
Ⓙ can't think of good places to hide

Writing Tell about something you hope you will never *fail* in. Be sure to use the word *fail* in your writing.

____

____

____

question

DAY 1

(noun) Something asked in order to get an answer or find out something.

*April asked a **question** about what parrots eat.*

question

DAY 2

(verb) To ask questions of someone or about something.

*Mr. Spears **questioned** the students about what they were reading.*

inquire • inquiry

DAY 3

inquire

(verb) To ask about someone or something.

*Augie **inquired** about his grade on the test.*

---

inquiry

(noun) A question or request for information.

*The principal answered an **inquiry** about after-school activities.*

inquiry

DAY 4

(noun) A study done to find answers to something.

*The school officials conducted an **inquiry** into attendance problems.*

Day 1 question

1. How would you complete this sentence? Say it aloud to a partner.

I like to ask questions when ________.

2. Which of the following sentences are *questions*? Circle your answers.

a. How many people live in Oklahoma?

b. Vermont became a state in 1791.

c. California has the largest population of any state.

d. When did Alaska become a state?

3. Rearrange the words in this sentence to turn it into a *question.* Write the *question* on the lines.

We are supposed to answer the question on the board.

____

____

Day 2 question

1. How would you complete this sentence? Say it aloud to a partner.

After reading, our teacher will question us about ________.

2. In which of these sentences is the word *question* <u>not</u> used correctly? Circle your answer.

a. The students question the teacher about the project.

b. Scientists question the causes of natural events.

c. The reporter questioned the mayor about the plans for a new park.

d. The group started a question into the cost of new books.

3. What do people do when they *question* someone? Circle your answer.

a. They make guesses.

b. They try to find out what the person knows.

c. They tell someone.

d. They don't care about the answers.

Day 3 inquire • inquiry

1. How would you complete these sentences? Say them aloud to a partner.

Something I might inquire about at a restaurant is ______.

For help with homework, I make an inquiry of ______.

2. In which sentence can *inquire* not take the place of "ask"? Circle your answer.

a. We called the train station to ask if the train had arrived.
b. When I see Grandma's friends, they always ask about her.
c. Damon hoped the teacher would ask him about snakes.
d. The principal stopped to ask why we were not in our classroom.

3. In which sentence could *inquiry* take the place of the word "question"? Circle your answer.

a. Maya had a question about the poem.
b. The letter came in answer to our question.
c. Our teacher answers every question we ask.
d. The first question on the test was the hardest.

Day 4 inquiry

1. How would you complete this sentence? Say it aloud to a partner.

I would like to make an inquiry into ______.

2. Which phrase best completes this sentence? Circle your answer.

A scientific inquiry found that ______.

a. Pluto was not a planet
b. country is the most popular music
c. there are many bicycles in China
d. Ramona Quimby is an interesting character

3. Which of these words has about the same meaning as *inquiry*? Circle your answer.

a. trace
b. opinion
c. study
d. subject

Day 5 question • inquire • inquiry

Fill in the bubble next to the correct answer.

1. Which sentence does not tell about a *question*?

Ⓐ It ends with a question mark.

Ⓑ It might start with "who," "what," "where," "when," "why," or "how."

Ⓒ You make a statement.

Ⓓ You ask one to find out something.

2. Which of these words does not mean about the same thing as *question*?

Ⓕ inquire

Ⓖ ask

Ⓗ understand

Ⓙ wonder

3. Which sentence uses the word *inquire* correctly?

Ⓐ The students wanted to inquire new library books.

Ⓑ You can inquire about overdue book fines at the front desk.

Ⓒ Most libraries inquire that people speak softly.

Ⓓ I will inquire Hilary to come with me to the library.

4. Which of these is a good subject for an official *inquiry*?

Ⓕ how schools spend their money

Ⓖ how many games each student owns

Ⓗ how many kids like ice cream

Ⓙ what kids' favorite toys are

Writing Think of a book character. What would you ask if you could *question* that character? Use one of this week's words in your writing.

____

____

____

contain

DAY 1

(verb) To hold or have within itself.

*This closet **contains** the art supplies.*

contain

DAY 2

(verb) To be made up of things.

*Some people cannot eat foods that **contain** nuts.*

consist

DAY 3

(verb) To be made up of; contain.

*Your homework today **consists** of math problems and a punctuation worksheet.*

include

DAY 4

(verb) To have or contain as part of the whole.

*Our school population **includes** teachers, students, and staff.*

Day 1 contain

1. How would you complete this sentence? Say it aloud to a partner.

My school bag contains ________.

2. Match each thing named on the left with what it *contains*. Draw lines to show your answers.

a. The ocean contains	articles and pictures.
b. A dictionary contains	people traveling somewhere.
c. A magazine contains	words and their meanings.
d. An airplane contains	different kinds of sea animals.

3. What could a big box *contain?* Write a sentence to answer the question. Be sure to include the word *contain.*

____

____

Day 2 contain

1. How would you complete this sentence? Say it aloud to a partner.

My favorite meal contains ________.

2. What two things do both of these snacks *contain?* Circle your answer.

Banana Berry Smoothie	Fruit Yogurt Salad
fresh berries	fresh berries
yogurt	melon
banana	yogurt

a. fresh berries and banana
b. yogurt and banana
c. fresh berries and melon
d. fresh berries and yogurt

3. In which sentence is the word *contain* used correctly? Circle your answer.

a. Contain your name on the test.
b. A song contains the band.
c. The speech contains many jokes.
d. Carrots contain in a salad.

Day 3 consist

1. How would you complete this sentence? Say it aloud to a partner.

My favorite dessert consists of these ingredients: ________.

2. What does each thing *consist* of? Draw lines to show your answers.

a. papier-mâché	animals, acrobats, clowns
b. a birthday party	cake, friends, presents
c. a circus	common interests, caring, shared times
d. a friendship	strips of paper, paste

3. Which sentence uses the word *consist* correctly? Circle your answer.

a. A healthy meal consists of more than one food group.
b. My crayon box does not consist of a red crayon.
c. If you consist, I will go with you to the movies.
d. How many marbles does the jar consist of?

Day 4 include

1. How would you complete this sentence? Say it aloud to a partner.

My whole family includes ________.

2. Match each group with the names of things *included* in that group. Draw lines to show your answers.

a. names of states	title, table of contents, index, glossary
b. kinds of trees	oceans, rivers, lakes, ponds
c. parts of a book	oak, maple, pine, redwood
d. bodies of water	Maine, Florida, Texas, Oregon

3. In which animal group would you *include* lizards and snakes? Circle your answer.

a. insects	c. fish
b. birds	d. reptiles

Day 5 contain • consist • include

Fill in the bubble next to the correct answer.

1. What is someone's school desk <u>not</u> likely to *contain*?

Ⓐ books

Ⓑ crayons

Ⓒ paper

Ⓓ a dog

2. Which of these foods does <u>not</u> *contain* fruit?

Ⓕ grape juice

Ⓖ strawberry ice cream

Ⓗ vegetable soup

Ⓙ blueberry yogurt

3. In which sentence could the phrase "*consists* of" take the place of "contains"?

Ⓐ A good book <u>contains</u> interesting characters and an exciting plot.

Ⓑ The drawer <u>contains</u> socks.

Ⓒ The aquarium <u>contains</u> three fish.

Ⓓ That paragraph <u>contains</u> many errors.

4. If you are included in a group, you ________.

Ⓕ are by yourself

Ⓖ must lead the others

Ⓗ must do what they say

Ⓙ are a member of the group

Writing Tell what books you would *include* in a list of your three favorite books. Be sure to use the word *include* in your writing.

____

____

____

produce
DAY 1

(verb) To build or make.

*The sun **produces** heat and light.*

productive
DAY 2

(adj.) Producing large amounts.

*Robertson's apple orchard is the most **productive** orchard in the county.*

product
DAY 3

(noun) Something that is made.

*Cheese and yogurt are dairy **products**.*

product
DAY 4

(noun) A result that follows from something else.

*Marcie's good grades were the **product** of hard work.*

Day 1 produce

1. How would you complete this sentence? Say it aloud to a partner.

I can use ________ to produce a ________.

2. In which sentence can the word *produce* take the place of "make"? Circle your answer.

a. Stephanie tells jokes to make people laugh.
b. American factories make millions of cars every year.
c. Some kids make money by doing jobs for their parents.
d. Strawberries make Tina break out in hives.

3. What does each of the things listed at the left *produce*? Draw lines to show your answers.

a. A whistle produces	a cool breeze.
b. A dairy produces	heat and light.
c. A campfire produces	milk, cheese, and ice cream.
d. A fan produces	a loud blast of sound.

Day 2 productive

1. How would you complete this sentence? Say it aloud to a partner.

I feel most productive when ________.

2. Which sentence describes a person who is *productive*? Circle your answer.

a. Felicia daydreamed about what she would do if she won the big prize.
b. Taylor meant to take her dog for a walk on Saturday.
c. Romero ate a sandwich for lunch every day this week.
d. Tran read three books and completed a book report on each one.

3. Which sentence can be completed with the word *productive*? Circle your answer.

a. Elias made ________ cookies for everyone on his birthday.
b. Penny ________ every word correctly on the spelling test.
c. Bailey's group stayed with the task and was the most ________.
d. Kayla said that our team had the best ________.

Day 3 product

1. How would you complete this sentence? Say it aloud to a partner.

One product that makes my life easier is ________.

2. Which of the following is <u>not</u> a *product*? Circle your answer.

a. apple juice
b. air
c. shoes
d. shampoo

3. In which sentence is the word *product* used correctly? Circle your answer.

a. The hotel was a smaller product of a famous castle in Spain.
b. The farm stand sells berries and products made from berries.
c. Passing out the workbooks is a regular classroom product.
d. Silly poems can sometimes be the products of stories.

Day 4 product

1. How would you complete this sentence? Say it aloud to a partner.

Having success at something is the product of ________.

2. Which phrase best completes this sentence? Circle your answer.

The class's science project was the product of ________.

a. the principal's announcement
b. dirt, seeds, and jars
c. the students' teamwork
d. first prize in the contest

3. In which sentence could the word *product* take the place of "result"? Circle your answer.

a. The argument was the <u>result</u> of a misunderstanding.
b. As a <u>result</u> of all the rain, the grass grew very fast.
c. The test <u>result</u> showed that the dog was sick.
d. We put a white flower in blue water and watched the <u>result</u>.

Day 5 produce • productive

Fill in the bubble next to the correct answer.

1. Which sentence does not use the word *produce* correctly?

Ⓐ Bells produce a bright, happy sound.
Ⓑ Our class will produce its own newspaper.
Ⓒ Some scientists produce that the Earth is getting warmer.
Ⓓ Power plants produce electricity.

2. A *productive* vegetable garden might ________.

Ⓕ have a fence around it
Ⓖ have a lot of weeds
Ⓗ not need any care
Ⓙ give a lot of tomatoes

3. Which of the following is the best definition for *product*?

Ⓐ something made in a kitchen
Ⓑ something made up of different things
Ⓒ something made by people or made in nature
Ⓓ something that occurs in nature

4. Winning the race was the *product* of ________.

Ⓕ good luck
Ⓖ months of training
Ⓗ good shoes
Ⓙ good weather for running

Writing Tell about a favorite *product* that your family buys and uses. Be sure to use the word *product* in your writing.

____

____

____

cause DAY 1

(noun) The reason why something happens.

*Warm temperatures were the **cause** of the snowman melting.*

cause DAY 2

(verb) To make something happen.

*A patch of ice **caused** the car to skid.*

effect DAY 3

(noun) Something produced by a cause.

*The forest fire was the **effect** of lightning striking several trees.*

effective DAY 4

(adj.) Able to bring about a result.

*The book fair was **effective** in raising money for new computers.*

Day 1 cause

1. How would you complete this sentence? Say it aloud to a partner.

_______ is always a cause for laughter.

2. Which of the following could be the *cause* of a fall? Circle your answers.

a. a bumpy sidewalk
b. a scraped knee
c. a broken arm
d. a wet and slippery floor

3. Which phrase best completes this sentence? Circle your answer.

The cause of the many large flowers was _______.

a. the gardener
b. picking the flowers
c. a month without rain
d. water, sunlight, and good soil

Day 2 cause

1. How would you complete this sentence? Say it aloud to a partner.

Thinking about lunch causes me to _______.

2. Which of these phrases could not complete this sentence? Circle your answer.

A giant snowstorm caused _______.

a. schools to be closed
b. cars to get stuck
c. flowers to bloom
d. people to stay at home

3. Which of these things might *cause* you to catch a cold? Circle your answer.

a. sneezing
b. eating good food
c. being near someone who has a cold
d. having a runny nose

Day 3 effect

1. How would you complete this sentence? Say it aloud to a partner.

One effect of reading is ________.

2. Match the causes at the left with the *effects* at the right. Draw lines to show your answers.

Cause	Effect
a. You eat too much food.	You stay home from school.
b. You get sick.	You get a blister on your foot.
c. A mosquito bites your arm.	You get an itchy bump.
d. You wear shoes that don't fit.	You get a stomachache.

3. Which of these things are *effects* of eating well and getting exercise? Circle your answers.

a. You stay healthy.
b. You get sick more often.
c. You spend more time watching TV.
d. Your body feels good.

Day 4 effective

1. How would you complete this sentence? Say it aloud to a partner.

One effective way to study spelling words is ________.

2. Which one best describes a plan that is *effective?* Circle your answer.

a. It is hard to understand.
b. It cannot be done.
c. It is not original.
d. It works.

3. Which sentence does <u>not</u> use the word *effective* correctly? Circle your answer.

a. E-mail is an effective way to stay in touch with friends.
b. Plain soap was not effective in removing the stain.
c. Every student had an effective copy of the worksheet.
d. The fan was effective in cooling the room.

Day 5 cause • effect • effective

Fill in the bubble next to the correct answer.

1. Which sentence uses the word *cause* correctly?

Ⓐ Missing the bus was the cause of Karin's oversleeping.
Ⓑ Jamie's smile was the cause of hearing a joke.
Ⓒ A flat tire was the cause of us missing soccer practice.
Ⓓ Shade in the summer was one cause of planting trees.

2. In which sentence could *causes* take the place of the underlined word?

Ⓕ The moon changes its appearance a little each night.
Ⓖ The Earth's rotation makes day and night.
Ⓗ Tad told us the reasons why he liked the book.
Ⓙ Being in a bad mood never excuses being rude.

3. The trash on the beach was the *effect* of ________.

Ⓐ people playing in the sand
Ⓑ a dirty beach
Ⓒ people not using trash cans
Ⓓ animals getting sick

4. Which word has about the same meaning as *effective?*

Ⓕ cause
Ⓖ scary
Ⓗ careless
Ⓙ useful

Writing Think about your favorite song. What *effect* does it have on you? Why does it *cause* this *effect?* Use the words *cause* and *effect* in your writing.

___

___

___

handle
DAY 1

(verb) To touch or hold with the hands.

*Be gentle when you **handle** the kitten.*

handle
DAY 2

(verb) To take care of a problem or situation; to deal with.

*Ms. Ruiz will **handle** putting the books on the shelves.*

control
DAY 3

(verb) To make someone or something do what you want; to direct.

*The principal **controls** the school schedule.*

control
DAY 4

(noun) Power over something.

*The principal has **control** over the school schedule.*

Day 1 handle

1. How would you complete this sentence? Say it aloud to a partner.

I am always very careful when I handle ______.

2. Which of these might be in a box with "*handle* with care" written on it? Circle your answers.

a. a glass vase
b. a pillow
c. a pair of shoes
d. a watch

3. Which phrase best completes this sentence? Circle your answer.

Before you handle food, you should ______.

a. take off your oven mitts
b. be sure the food is clean
c. take it out of the refrigerator
d. make sure your hands are clean

Day 2 handle

1. How would you complete this sentence? Say it aloud to a partner.

When ______ asked me to ______, I knew I could handle it.

2. In which sentence can the underlined words not be replaced by *handle*? Circle your answer.

a. Ms. Dowd will take charge of all the arrangements for the party.
b. Barry was sure that he could be successful in the job.
c. Please turn in your test paper when you have finished.
d. The whole family trusted Dad to take care of everything.

3. Which of these jobs do you think you could *handle*? Circle your answers.

a. being a doctor
b. picking flowers
c. feeding a pet
d. building a house

Day 3 control

1. How would you complete this sentence? Say it aloud to a partner.

I wish I had a device to control ________.

2. Which phrase best completes this sentence? Circle your answer.

Brianna tried to control the book club by ________.

a. letting everyone talk at once
b. making up lots of rules
c. never coming to meetings
d. asking the teacher questions

3. Which of these things do people *control*? Circle your answers.

a. what they choose to buy at the store
b. when it will rain
c. what they do in their free time
d. when the sun comes up

Day 4 control

1. How would you complete this sentence? Say it aloud to a partner.

My parents have control over ________.

2. Match each person with what he or she takes *control* of. Draw lines to show your answers.

a. A pilot	takes control of fires.
b. A firefighter	has control over the players.
c. A coach	takes control of a group.
d. A leader	has control over a plane.

3. List three things you have *control* over.

a. ______________________________

b. ______________________________

c. ______________________________

Day 5 handle • control

Fill in the bubble next to the correct answer.

1. Which sentence uses the word *handle* correctly?

Ⓐ The teacher asked Jake to handle him the report.
Ⓑ Monica doesn't like to handle anything that's wet and slimy.
Ⓒ Everyone handled their tickets to the man at the door.
Ⓓ It's Shandra's turn to handle out the worksheets.

2. Which statement tells what it means to *handle* a problem?

Ⓕ You hand it off to someone else.
Ⓖ You make trouble.
Ⓗ You take care of things.
Ⓙ You write down everything that happens.

3. The bus driver *controls* the bus by ________.

Ⓐ sitting in front
Ⓑ owning it
Ⓒ parking it in front of the school
Ⓓ steering it and using the brakes

4. Which sentence is <u>not</u> true?

Ⓕ A principal has control over how a school is run.
Ⓖ Teachers have control over what their students do in class.
Ⓗ A librarian has control over what is written in books.
Ⓙ Parents can have some control over what their children watch on TV.

Writing What is the hardest task you have *handled?* Tell what you did to *handle* it. Be sure to use the word *handle* in your sentence.

____

____

____

recall DAY 1

(verb) To remember something.

*Mom couldn't **recall** the name of the bookstore.*

recount DAY 2

(verb) To tell about something that happened.

*The guest speaker will **recount** his adventures in Africa.*

memorize • recite DAY 3

memorize

(verb) To learn something by heart.

*Jana has **memorized** all her friends' phone numbers.*

---

recite

(verb) To say aloud something you have memorized.

*Husna can **recite** all fifty state capitals.*

recite DAY 4

(verb) To list or tell about in detail.

*James **recited** a long list of people who came to his party.*

Day 1 recall

1. How would you complete this sentence? Say it aloud to a partner.

I recall that we learned about ________ yesterday.

2. In which sentence can you not use *recall* in place of "remember"? Circle your answer.

a. Caitlin couldn't remember the words to the song.
b. It's fun to remember the good times we had on vacation.
c. Did you remember to turn out the light?
d. I think I know that girl, but I can't remember her name.

3. What can you *recall* about the last book you read? Write three things about it.

a. ____

b. ____

c. ____

Day 2 recount

1. How would you complete this sentence? Say it aloud to a partner.

I like to recount the time I ________.

2. Which of the following describes *recounting* something? Circle your answers.

a. telling the story of something that happened to you
b. remembering what was on a lost shopping list
c. reciting the words to a favorite song
d. telling your family about your day at school

3. Which sentence can you complete with the word *recount*? Circle your answer.

a. Our teacher can ________ the names of all her students.
b. Bao couldn't ________ where he'd left his jacket.
c. Joni tries to ________ a new poem every week.
d. Alison's report will ________ the story of Christopher Columbus.

Daily Academic Vocabulary

Day 3 memorize • recite

1. How would you complete these sentences? Say them aloud to a partner.

I have memorized a ________.

I will recite it to ________.

2. Which of these things would someone be likely to *memorize*? Circle your answers.

a. lines from a play

b. a whole chapter from a book

c. the words to a song

d. parts of the phone book

3. Write the first two lines of a song or poem that you have *memorized* and can recite.

____

____

____

Day 4 recite

1. How would you complete this sentence? Say it aloud to a partner.

A list that I could recite is ________.

2. Which phrases could complete the sentence? Circle your answers.

We listened to Bibi recite ________.

a. a long list of things she had to do

b. her bike

c. the names of all the states

d. her idea for the project

3. Which sentence could not be completed with the word *recite*? Circle your answer.

a. Kirby likes to ________ facts about baseball players.

b. Sarah likes to ________ all the places she went on vacation.

c. Serena likes to ________ the names of all her pets.

d. Fred likes to ________ copying animal sounds.

Day 5 recall • recount • memorize • recite

Fill in the bubble next to the correct answer.

1. When you *recall* a detail, you ________.

Ⓐ rewrite it
Ⓑ take it out of your story
Ⓒ remember it
Ⓓ decide if it's important or not

2. If you *recount* an adventure, you ________.

Ⓕ tell about it
Ⓖ make it up in your head
Ⓗ change your story about it
Ⓙ remember something you have read

3. Which sentence could you complete with the word *memorize*?

Ⓐ Fiona was eager to ________ the new movie.
Ⓑ Mom helped Audra ________ her part in the play.
Ⓒ Carlo couldn't ________ how he spent his birthday money.
Ⓓ We listened to Evan ________ his trumpet.

4. In which sentence is the word *recite* <u>not</u> used correctly?

Ⓕ Danielle can recite the names of all twelve of her cousins.
Ⓖ Angela taught her little sister to recite the alphabet.
Ⓗ Iman has watched the movie so often he can recite parts of it.
Ⓙ Desmond needs to recite his dance for the school show.

Writing Explain why you might need to *memorize* something. Be sure to use the word *memorize* in your writing.

____

____

____

REVIEW: Weeks 19–26

Daily Academic Vocabulary

attempted	consisted	decide	fail	produced
consider	control	effective	memorize	recite

Day 1

Fill in the blanks with words from the word box.

Many people ________________ Thomas Edison to be the inventor of the light bulb. He wasn't. He invented the first light bulb that ________________ light safely. This invention provided an ________________ way to light homes and businesses without using candles or gas. He also formed an electrical power company to ________________ getting electricity to homes.

Day 2

Fill in the blanks with words from the word box.

Byrne's teacher asked everyone to ________________ a poem. They had a week to learn their poem. Then they had to ________________ their poem for the whole class. Byrne couldn't ________________ which poem to choose. His favorite poem ________________ of many stanzas. If he ________________ to learn a really long poem, he was afraid he might ________________. He practiced and studied his poem every day. He was a success!

REVIEW: Weeks 19–26

Daily Academic Vocabulary

cause	include	products	recall	failure
contains	inquiry	questions	recount	

Day 3

Fill in the blanks with words from the word box.

It's a good idea to read the labels on food ________________. Reading the label will answer ________________ about what the food ________________. Things like nuts can ________________ problems for some people. ________________ to read labels might lead to people eating something they shouldn't.

Day 4

Fill in the blanks with words from the word box.

Suppose someone asked you to ________________ to them what happened at school yesterday. How would you respond to that ________________? What would you say? Would you tell everything that you could ________________, or just the important things? If you told only the important things, what events would you ________________?

Day 5

Crack the Code!

Write one of the words from the word box on the lines beneath each clue.

attempt	decide	failure	inquiry	question
cause	decision	handle	memorize	recall
consider	effect	include	produce	recite
contain	effective	inquire	product	recount
control	fail			

1. When you make up your mind, this is the result.

___ ___ ___ ___(1) ___(2) ___ ___ ___

2. to try to do something

___(3) ___ ___ ___ ___ ___(4) ___

3. what you do when you learn something by heart

___ ___ ___ ___(5) ___ ___ ___ ___

4. what you do when you ask for information

___ ___ ___ ___ ___ ___ ___(6)

5. something caused by something else

___ ___ ___ ___ ___ ___(7)

6. what you make when you ask for information

___ ___(8) ___ ___ ___ ___(9) ___

Now use the numbers under the letters to crack the code. Write the letters on the lines below. The words will complete this quotation.

Thomas Edison said, "Genius is 1 percent inspiration and 99 percent _____."

___(4) ___(6) ___(9) ___(2) ___(4) ___(1) ___(9) ___(3) ___(7) ___(1) ___(5) ___(8)

Words for Weeks 28–35

Week 28
term
label

Week 29
conduct
operate
process

Week 30
view
approach

Week 31
content
contents
feature

Week 32
purpose
object
objective

Week 33
judge
judgment
prove
disprove
proof

Week 34
assist
assistance
cooperate
cooperation

Week 35
expect
predict
prediction
predictable

term
DAY 1

(noun) A word having a specific meaning.

*The **terms** "note" and "rest" have special meanings in music.*

label
DAY 2

(noun) A tag or sticker that is attached to an object and gives useful information.

*The **label** on the cereal box tells what is inside.*

(verb) To attach a label to an object.

*We will **label** the boxes so we know what is inside.*

label
DAY 3

(noun) A word or phrase that describes someone or something.

*The drawing of the sailboat had **labels** that told the name of each part.*

label
DAY 4

(verb) To write the names of parts or items.

*We drew a picture of a spider and **labeled** the parts of its body.*

Day 1 term

1. How would you complete this sentence? Say it aloud to a partner.

"Mouse," "Web site," and ________ are a few computer terms I know.

2. Which group of words are *terms* you know from math? Circle your answer.

a. noun, verb, adjective
b. sum, multiply, subtract
c. download, memory, software
d. mammal, habitat, predator

3. Which sentence correctly uses the word *term*? Circle your answer.

a. A library is a term where you can borrow books.
b. Fred made a term of the city out of cardboard boxes.
c. "Nocturnal" is a term that means "active at night."
d. A star is a term in the night sky.

Day 2 label

1. How would you complete these sentences? Say them aloud to a partner.

The label on a food container tells ________.

We label things in our classroom so that ________.

2. Which of these things usually have *labels*? Circle your answers.

a.

b.

c.

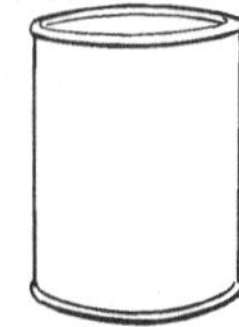
d.

3. Why might you *label* a box or jar? Circle your answer.

a. so you can close it tightly
b. so whatever is inside will keep better
c. so you know what is inside
d. to make it look nice

Day 3 label

1. How would you complete this sentence? Say it aloud to a partner.

Labels on a diagram of our school would help new students ________.

2. Draw lines to connect the *labels* with the correct parts of the illustration.

Molly Logan
532 Union St.
Barre, VT 05578

Ms. Wendy Hill
3700 Cascades Dr.
Portland, OR 95478

stamp

return address

address

3. Which *labels* might you put on a drawing of a butterfly? Circle your answers.

a. head

b. wing

c. flipper

d. teeth

Day 4 label

1. How would you complete this sentence? Say it aloud to a partner.

If I drew a picture of a tiger, I would label ________.

2. In which sentence is the word *label* used correctly? Circle your answer.

a. The teacher showed us how to label a butterfly out of paper.

b. We will label the room with paper airplanes.

c. For the test, we had to label the parts of a caterpillar.

d. Gina's job is to label the party.

3. Which of these things might you *label?* Circle your answers.

a. places on a map in a book

b. the parts of a letter you write

c. a picture you hang on your wall

d. the parts of an octopus in a drawing

Day 5 term • label

Fill in the bubble next to the correct answer.

1. Which sentence uses the word *term* correctly?

Ⓐ Friendliness is a term of many dogs, cats, and other pets.
Ⓑ Recycle is a term for making new things from old ones.
Ⓒ Fairness is a term all teachers should have.
Ⓓ A term is a label on a picture.

2. Which of these things would be least likely to have a *label*?

Ⓕ a milk jug
Ⓖ a watermelon
Ⓗ a jar of peanut butter
Ⓙ a box of crackers

3. Why would you put *labels* on a drawing?

Ⓐ to tell what the parts are
Ⓑ to tell how you did it
Ⓒ to tell why you drew it
Ⓓ to give the picture a name

4. If you *labeled* objects in the classroom, you would ______.

Ⓕ tell what everything is made of
Ⓖ put a student's name on every object
Ⓗ put a sign on each object that tells its name
Ⓙ group them by size and color

Writing Tell why you think *labels* are useful and important. Be sure to use the word *label* in your writing.

____

____

____

conduct
DAY 1

(verb) To manage or direct the course of something.

*The museum **conducted** a study to find out which exhibits people liked best.*

(verb) To lead or guide.

*The principal **conducts** a tour of the school for new students.*

operate
DAY 2

(verb) To work or run.

*The TV won't **operate** if it's not plugged in.*

operate
DAY 3

(verb) To control the running of something.

*I **operate** the TV when we use it in class.*

process
DAY 4

(noun) A series of actions that make something.

*We are learning the **process** of writing a good story.*

Day 1 conduct

1. How would you complete these sentences? Say them aloud to a partner.

I would like to conduct an experiment on ________.

I think it would be fun to conduct a tour of ________.

2. Which of these things could someone *conduct*? Circle your answers.

a. a dictionary
b. an investigation
c. a survey
d. dinner

3. In which sentence could *conduct* take the place of "lead"? Circle your answer.

a. Clues sometimes <u>lead</u> you to the wrong conclusion.
b. Mr. Holland will <u>lead</u> a tour of the public gardens.
c. All three paths <u>lead</u> to the same place.
d. The mayor's float will <u>lead</u> the parade.

Day 2 operate

1. How would you complete this sentence? Say it aloud to a partner.

________ is something in my home that uses batteries to operate.

2. Name three things that *operate* on electricity.

a. ________________________________

b. ________________________________

c. ________________________________

3. Which of these things *operate* by wind power? Circle your answers.

a. a flashlight
b. a kite
c. a sailboat
d. a microwave

Day 3 operate

1. How would you complete this sentence? Say it aloud to a partner.

When I grow up, I would like to operate a ________.

2. Which of these things can you *operate* now? Circle your answers.

a. a bike
b. a helicopter
c. a school bus
d. a computer

3. In which of these sentences could *operate* not take the place of "run"? Circle your answer.

a. The Andersons run a farm stand on Route 32.
b. Peter's older brother will run in a 5K race.
c. You need to be careful when you run any kind of machine.
d. The school buses do not run on weekends.

Day 4 process

1. How would you complete this sentence? Say it aloud to a partner.

In school, I have learned the process of ________.

2. Which phrase best completes this sentence? Circle your answer.

The scientific process ________.

a. makes science
b. tells you facts about the solar system
c. uses specific actions to answer a scientific question
d. uses guessing to answer a scientific question

3. Which *process* would you use to decide which movie to watch with your friends? Circle your answer.

a. voting process
b. number process
c. writing process
d. scientific process

Day 5 conduct • operate • process

Fill in the bubble next to the correct answer.

1. If you *conduct* a meeting, you ________.

Ⓐ do all the talking
Ⓑ listen and say nothing
Ⓒ lead it and direct it
Ⓓ invite your friends to come

2. Which sentence uses the word *operate* correctly?

Ⓕ The refrigerator operates very quietly.
Ⓖ This road operates alongside the river.
Ⓗ The idea operated through her mind.
Ⓙ The story will operate in all the newspapers.

3. You press a button to *operate* ________.

Ⓐ a suitcase
Ⓑ a picnic basket
Ⓒ a phone
Ⓓ a drawer

4. Which number *process* is used to solve this problem: 3 × 5 = ________?

Ⓕ addition
Ⓖ division
Ⓗ multiplication
Ⓙ subtraction

Writing Imagine you had a chance to *conduct* a tour. Where would you like to *conduct* it? Tell about the place and why you would like to show others around it. Use the word *conduct* in your writing.

____

____

____

view DAY 1

(noun) What you see from where you are. *The house has a **view** of the lake.*

(verb) To see or look at. *Our class **viewed** the jellyfish exhibit the day it opened at the aquarium.*

approach DAY 2

(verb) To move nearer. *The children will **approach** the dog carefully.*

approach DAY 3

(verb) To begin or prepare to work on something. *How will you **approach** the word problem?*

approach DAY 4

(noun) A way of dealing with something. *When we didn't understand the new math concept, our teacher tried a different **approach**.*

Day 1 view

1. How would you complete these sentences? Say them aloud to a partner.

My favorite view is the one from ________.

I would like to view ________.

2. Which words might describe the *view* from a mountaintop? Circle your answers.

a. beautiful
b. small
c. ordinary
d. breathtaking

3. Where would you go to *view* these things? Draw lines to show your answers.

a. waves crashing on the beach	an art museum
b. paintings and drawings	a city park
c. dinosaur bones	the seashore
d. people jogging and skating	a natural history museum

Day 2 approach

1. How would you complete this sentence? Say it aloud to a partner.

I always slow down when I approach ________.

2. Which sentence uses the word *approach* correctly? Circle your answer.

a. Our campsite approached a clearing in the woods.
b. We woke up as soon as the sun approached in the sky.
c. We saw a deer and a fawn approach the clearing.
d. They ran away as soon as they approached us nearby.

3. Which of these things are you glad to see *approach*? Circle your answers.

a. your birthday
b. a visit to the doctor for shots
c. a big test
d. summer vacation

Day 3 approach

1. How would you complete this sentence? Say it aloud to a partner.

I always approach my schoolwork by ______.

2. Which phrases best complete this sentence? Circle your answers.

The best way to approach a problem is ______.

a. to think it cannot be solved
b. to believe it can be solved
c. to look at all sides of the problem
d. to understand just a small part of the problem

3. What are two things you do when you *approach* writing a story?

a. ______________________________

b. ______________________________

Day 4 approach

1. How would you complete this sentence? Say it aloud to a partner.

One approach to memorizing a poem is ______.

2. Which phrase best completes this sentence? Circle your answer.

If you have a new approach to a problem, you ______.

a. have a problem no one else has ever had
b. think of a different way to deal with it
c. do what everyone else does
d. do what you always do

3. Which one do you think is the best *approach* to studying for a spelling test? Circle your answer.

a. Study right before the test.
b. Watch TV while you study.
c. Quickly read the words.
d. Read and write the words every day.

Day 5 view • approach

Fill in the bubble next to the correct answer.

1. In which sentence is the word *view* not used correctly?

Ⓐ Everyone was eager to view the new movie.
Ⓑ The hotel room had a view of the park.
Ⓒ We could not view if the bike had a flat tire.
Ⓓ From the plane, we had a great view of the city at night.

2. If you are *approaching* your ninth birthday, ______.

Ⓕ you are already nine
Ⓖ you are worrying about it
Ⓗ your birthday is getting closer
Ⓙ your birthday already happened

3. If you are *approaching* a problem, you are ______.

Ⓐ figuring out how to deal with it
Ⓑ getting closer to it
Ⓒ trying to get away from it
Ⓓ pretending there is no problem

4. You might try a different *approach*, if ______.

Ⓕ your old methods always work
Ⓖ you don't like what you have to do
Ⓗ you don't know what you want to do
Ⓙ you didn't have success the first time

Writing Explain your favorite *approach* to dealing with hiccups. Be sure to use the word *approach* in your writing.

____

____

____

content
DAY 1

(noun) The information that is in a book or other written work.

*The **content** of the magazine is all about nature.*

contents
DAY 2

(noun) The things found inside something, such as a container.

*Because the label came off the can, nobody knows its **contents**.*

feature
DAY 3

(noun) An important part or quality of something.

*Clues are always an important **feature** of a mystery story.*

feature
DAY 4

(verb) To give special attention to.

*The magazine **featured** the story about the rainforest.*

Day 1 content

1. How would you complete this sentence? Say it aloud to a partner.

I would choose a library book that had content about ________.

2. What kind of textbook would have this *content*? Circle your answer.

• *How Things Move* • *How Plants Make Food* • *Rocks and Minerals*

a. science
b. language arts
c. social studies
d. health

3. Which of these things would not be part of the *content* of a reading book? Circle your answer.

a. stories
b. math problems
c. poems
d. nonfiction articles

Day 2 contents

1. How would you complete this sentence? Say it aloud to a partner.

The contents of my bedroom include ________.

2. What do you think are the *contents* of this bag? Circle your answer.

a. zipper, straps, student
b. dog, cat, hamster
c. books, homework, pencils
d. school, home, library

3. What do you think are the *contents* of this basket? Circle your answer.

a. clothes hangers
b. books
c. washing machine
d. dirty clothes

Day 3 feature

1. How would you complete this sentence? Say it aloud to a partner.

My favorite feature of our community is _______.

2. List two *features* that make a big city different from a small town.

a. ______________________________

b. ______________________________

3. Which one is not a *feature* of a map? Circle your answer.

a. shows you where things are
b. a key or legend
c. a computer
d. helps you get from one place to another

Day 4 feature

1. How would you complete this sentence? Say it aloud to a partner.

If I wrote a play, I would feature a part for _______.

2. Which phrase best completes this sentence? Circle your answer.

A school newspaper would feature _______.

a. articles written by scientists
b. stories and articles by students
c. state and national news
d. weather reports from around the world

3. In which sentence is the word *feature* used correctly? Circle your answer.

a. The science fair will feature our class's science project.
b. An article about Mars features the magazine.
c. Mars is featured by its red glow in the night sky.
d. Mars is commonly feature "The Red Planet."

Day 5 content • contents • feature

Fill in the bubble next to the correct answer.

1. Which of these things does not have *content*?

Ⓐ a Web site
Ⓑ a book
Ⓒ a blank notebook
Ⓓ a magazine

2. Which of these would not be among the *contents* of the art supply closet?

Ⓕ pairs of scissors
Ⓖ paintbrushes
Ⓗ a pair of rubber boots
Ⓙ colored construction paper

3. In which sentence could you use the word *feature* to fill in the blank?

Ⓐ The children's room is the best ________ of our library.
Ⓑ A library card is a ________ for checking out books.
Ⓒ There is a ________ if you return a book late.
Ⓓ The ________ tells you where to find a book.

4. If an actor is *featured* on a TV show, she ________.

Ⓕ has a very small part
Ⓖ is seen but doesn't speak
Ⓗ appears in the first 3 minutes
Ⓙ has a large part

Writing What is one *feature* of your favorite book? Why do you like it so much? Be sure to use the word *feature* in your writing.

___

___

___

purpose
DAY 1

(noun) The reason something exists; its use.

*The **purpose** of this button is to turn on the computer.*

purpose
DAY 2

(noun) The reason why something is done.

*The **purpose** of the meeting was to plan the school fair.*

object
DAY 3

(noun) Something that can be seen and felt, but is not alive.

*Marcie spotted a shiny **object** in the sand.*

objective
DAY 4

(noun) Something that one tries to achieve; purpose.

*The **objective** of our project is to learn about sharks.*

Day 1 purpose

1. How would you complete this sentence? Say it aloud to a partner.

For me, the purpose of a phone is to ______.

2. Connect each object with its *purpose.* Draw lines to show your answers.

a. a light switch	to lock and unlock a door
b. a key	to turn lights on and off
c. a water faucet	to write something down
d. a pencil	to control the flow of water

3. Which phrase best completes this sentence? Circle your answer.

The purpose of an umbrella is to ______.

a. match your raincoat
b. bring bad luck if you open it indoors
c. prevent you from getting wet in the rain
d. lend it to a friend

Day 2 purpose

1. How would you complete this sentence? Say it aloud to a partner.

My purpose for writing a book report is ______.

2. Which sentence correctly uses the word *purpose*? Circle your answer.

a. Oversleeping was my purpose for being late.
b. My purpose for calling is to ask about our homework.
c. Studying hard is the purpose I did well on the test.
d. He had no purpose to lie about what happened.

3. What do you think is your teacher's *purpose* for giving you homework?

____

____

Day 3 object

1. How would you complete this sentence? Say it aloud to a partner.

My favorite object in this room is ______ because ______.

2. List a different *object* that you might use in each of these subjects.

a. science ____________________

b. social studies ____________________

c. art ____________________

d. math ____________________

3. Which of the following things is not an *object*? Circle your answer.

a. a water bottle
b. a cage
c. a hamster
d. a running wheel

Day 4 objective

1. How would you complete this sentence? Say it aloud to a partner.

My objective in school is ______.

2. Which phrase best completes this sentence? Circle your answer.

The objective of the student art sale is ______.

a. next Saturday and Sunday
b. to raise money for more art supplies
c. in the school gym
d. my favorite school day

3. If your *objective* is to grow a sweet potato vine, you need ______. Circle your answer.

a. a sweet potato, a jar, and water
b. a fork, salt, and butter
c. to bake a sweet potato
d. to like sweet potatoes

Day 5 purpose • object • objective

Fill in the bubble next to the correct answer.

1. The *purpose* of a doorknob is ________.

Ⓐ to decorate the door
Ⓑ to open a door
Ⓒ for you to hang your jacket on it
Ⓓ to be a shiny object

2. Which of the following is <u>not</u> a *purpose* for going to the library?

Ⓕ to mail a letter
Ⓖ to find a book about dolphins
Ⓗ to return a book you borrowed
Ⓙ to check out books to read for fun

3. Which sentence could <u>not</u> be completed with the word *object*?

Ⓐ Rob found the ________ he was looking for.
Ⓑ Which ________ did you find on the ground?
Ⓒ The parakeet stared at its ________ in the mirror.
Ⓓ Thalia chose the ________ she liked best.

4. Which sentence uses the word *objective* correctly?

Ⓕ The woman objective to the store's prices.
Ⓖ Our objective was to get to the airport on time.
Ⓗ If no one has objective, we can start tomorrow.
Ⓙ Ben slipped the objective into his pocket.

Writing Tell about an *objective* you might have if you went on a hike. Be sure to use the word *objective* in your writing.

____

____

____

judge • judgment DAY 1

judge

(verb) To form an opinion about something. *They bought the car they **judged** to be the safest.*

---

judgment

(noun) An opinion about someone or something. *He tries not to make a **judgment** about people he's just met.*

judgment DAY 2

(noun) The ability to make wise choices. *We trusted Mom's **judgment** in all important matters.*

prove • disprove DAY 3

prove

(verb) To show that something is true. *Can you **prove** that pencil is yours?*

---

disprove

(verb) To show that something is false. *Beth **disproved** the idea that boys run faster than girls by winning the race.*

proof DAY 4

(noun) Facts or evidence that something is true. *Emma's grades were **proof** she worked hard in school.*

Day 1 judge • judgment

1. How would you complete these sentences? Say them aloud to a partner.

I try not to judge people until ________.

Before I make a judgment about a book, I will ________.

2. An old saying is, "Don't *judge* a book by its cover." What does this mean? Circle your answer.

a. Don't choose a book for a judge unless it has a nice cover.
b. Don't weigh a book without including its cover.
c. Don't form an opinion based only on what you can first see.
d. Don't write a book report if all you've read is the cover.

3. Which of these situations require making a *judgment*? Circle your answers.

a. selecting a new pair of shoes
b. deciding who can be trusted with a secret
c. eating lunch
d. waiting for the school bus

Day 2 judgment

1. How would you complete this sentence? Say it aloud to a partner.

I think I have good judgment when it comes to ________.

2. In which sentence is the word *judgment* used correctly? Circle your answer.

a. The teacher had a calm and caring judgment.
b. Elias showed good judgment when he chose his team.
c. Loyalty is a common judgment of a dog.
d. Celia made a strong judgment for going to the water park.

3. Which of these actions would you say shows good *judgment*? Circle your answer.

a. staying up late on a school night
b. riding your bike on a crowded sidewalk
c. petting a strange dog
d. choosing healthy snacks

Day 3 prove • disprove

1. How would you complete these sentences? Say them aloud to a partner.

I can prove ________ by ________.

I can disprove that I am only five years old by ________.

2. Circle the statements you could *prove*. Underline the statements you could *disprove*.

a. Wood floats.

b. A feather falls faster than a rock.

c. Plants need water and light.

d. Yellow and red make blue.

3. Which of these sentences do <u>not</u> use *prove* or *disprove* correctly? Circle your answers.

a. Mother disproves when we yell in the house.

b. The experiment proves that oil floats on water.

c. I set out to disprove her claim that she was the fastest runner.

d. The fingerprints are prove that someone touched the wet paint.

Day 4 proof

1. How would you complete this sentence? Say it aloud to a partner.

The work I do in school is proof that I ________.

2. What would be *proof* for each of the statements at the left? Draw lines to show your answers.

a. Deer ate the flowers.	measuring the sides
b. The triangle has three equal sides.	dried mud on his shoes
c. David stepped in a mud puddle.	a stuffy nose and coughing
d. Amelia has a cold.	deer tracks in the flower bed

3. Which ones show *proof* that you finished your homework? Circle your answers.

a. Your teacher checked it.

b. You put your books away.

c. A parent made sure you did it.

d. You decided to watch TV.

Day 5 judge • judgment prove • disprove • proof

Fill in the bubble next to the correct answer.

1. If you *judge* something, then you ________.

Ⓐ decide that it's bad

Ⓑ enter it in a contest

Ⓒ form an opinion about it

Ⓓ choose it over other things

2. In which sentence could *judgment* take the place of the underlined word?

Ⓕ We trust Dad's <u>opinion</u> when it comes to food.

Ⓖ Our book club made the <u>decision</u> to meet on Thursday.

Ⓗ The successful science fair was the <u>result</u> of careful planning.

Ⓙ Tomika used her <u>imagination</u> to picture a beautiful white sand beach.

3. Which of the following is something you <u>cannot</u> *prove* or *disprove*?

Ⓐ an answer in math

Ⓑ a science fact

Ⓒ an opinion

Ⓓ that something happened

4. The empty milk carton is *proof* that ________.

Ⓕ milk is good for your bones

Ⓖ everyone should drink milk

Ⓗ milk should come in bottles

Ⓙ someone drank the last of the milk

Writing What is something you can *prove?* How can you *prove* it? Be sure to use the word *prove* in your writing.

____

____

____

assist
DAY 1

(verb) To help or give aid to someone.

*Jenna **assisted** the teacher by putting away the art supplies.*

assistance
DAY 2

(noun) Help or aid.

*Everyone offered **assistance** to clean up the room.*

cooperate
DAY 3

(verb) To work together.

*The students should **cooperate** during their group project.*

cooperation
DAY 4

(noun) The act of working together.

*The **cooperation** of the team members helped them win the game.*

Day 1 assist

1. How would you complete this sentence? Say it aloud to a partner.

I am happy to assist anyone who ______.

2. Which of these jobs could you *assist* with at home? Circle your answers.

a. preparing meals
b. washing the dishes
c. feeding a pet
d. washing the clothes

3. Which phrase best completes this sentence? Circle your answer.

We can assist the teacher by ______.

a. talking all at once
b. listening and following directions
c. being mean to our classmates
d. not doing our work

Day 2 assistance

1. How would you complete this sentence? Say it aloud to a partner.

I need an adult's assistance in order to ______.

2. In which sentence is the word *assistance* not used correctly? Circle your answer.

a. We needed assistance when we got a flat tire.
b. Moira did her homework without assistance from anyone.
c. The assistance crowd cheered for the team.
d. I needed assistance when I was learning to ride my bike.

3. What can you do with *assistance* and without *assistance*? Write some examples.

What I Can Do with Assistance	What I Can Do without Assistance
a. ______________________	a. ______________________
b. ______________________	b. ______________________
c. ______________________	c. ______________________

Day 3 cooperate

1. How would you complete this sentence? Say it aloud to a partner.

I often cooperate with ________ to ________.

2. Which people on the left need to *cooperate* with the people on the right? Draw lines to show your answers.

a. the school principal	other people in government
b. the president of a country	other members of the team
c. the captain of a basketball team	the director of a play
d. actors	teachers

3. In which sentence is the word *cooperate* used correctly? Circle your answer.

a. Kylie knew she could cooperate on her own.
b. Justin and Colin knew they must cooperate to finish on time.
c. The teacher told the group she was happy with their cooperate.
d. Dan cooperated when he took the pen away from Selene.

Day 4 cooperation

1. How would you complete this sentence? Say it aloud to a partner.

It takes cooperation to ________.

2. Which phrase correctly describes *cooperation*? Circle your answer.

a. working together
b. making others do things
c. performing surgery
d. doing everything yourself

3. Which sentence correctly describes an act of *cooperation*? Circle your answer.

a. Shana watched her brother make his bed.
b. Mr. Clark told the students how to complete the project.
c. Marie searched the Internet for information.
d. Alex helped Adrian finish his chores so they could go to the park.

Day 5 **assist • assistance** **cooperate • cooperation**

Fill in the bubble next to the correct answer.

1. If you *assist* someone, you ______.

Ⓐ invite the person to your home
Ⓑ help the person do something
Ⓒ try to make the person agree with you
Ⓓ try to keep out of the person's way

2. Which of these words could <u>not</u> take the place of *assistance* in a sentence?

Ⓕ help
Ⓖ aid
Ⓗ bother
Ⓙ support

Cooperation is always important!

3. Which word does <u>not</u> complete this sentence correctly?

When you cooperate, you ______.

Ⓐ help
Ⓑ aid
Ⓒ support
Ⓓ change

4. In which sentence could *cooperation* be used to fill in the blank?

Ⓕ The teacher insisted on ______ among the students.
Ⓖ The project required that ______ be the result of one student.
Ⓗ The team ______ to win the game.
Ⓙ Do the ______ homework on your own.

Writing Describe the last time you *cooperated* with someone on a school project. Be sure to use one of this week's words in your writing.

____

____

____

expect DAY 1

(verb) To think that an event or action is likely to happen.

*We **expect** Grandma to visit next week.*

predict DAY 2

(verb) To tell in advance what you think will happen in the future.

*I **predict** that it will rain tomorrow.*

prediction DAY 3

(noun) An event that is told before it happens.

*It is my **prediction** that our team will win.*

predictable DAY 4

(adj.) Happening in a way or at a time in which you could have expected.

*Recess is **predictable** because it happens at the same time every day.*

Day 1 expect

1. How would you complete this sentence? Say it aloud to a partner.

I expect a funny movie to ________.

2. Study this pattern. If the pattern continued, what shape would you *expect* to come next? Circle your answer.

○ ☆ ◇ ♡ ◇ ☆ ○ ☆ ◇ ♡ ◇ ☆ ○ ☆ ◇ ♡ ◇ ☆ ○ ☆ ◇

a. ○ b. ☆ c. ◇ d. ♡

3. In which sentence is *expect* <u>not</u> used correctly? Circle your answer.

a. Good teachers expect all their students to learn.
b. We expect to get our book reports back today.
c. Someone should expect the bike to be sure it's safe.
d. We expect to leave on vacation in six weeks.

Day 2 predict

1. How would you complete this sentence? Say it aloud to a partner.

I predict that this afternoon at 5 o'clock, I will ________.

2. *Predict* something that will happen on each of these days. Write what you *predict*.

a. tomorrow ______________________________

b. Saturday ______________________________

c. Monday ______________________________

3. Which phrase best completes this sentence? Circle your answer.

When you predict while reading, you ________.

a. think about what will happen when you stop reading
b. try to figure out what will happen next in the story
c. try to decide if you like the story
d. think about who else has read this book

Day 3 prediction

1. How would you complete this sentence? Say it aloud to a partner.

My prediction for this summer is that ______.

2. Which one of these statements is a *prediction*? Circle your answer.

a. The library always has a summer reading program.
b. Every year there is a different topic.
c. This year's topic is "Adventuring with Books."
d. I think we're going to read some exciting books.

3. In which sentence is the word *prediction* used correctly? Circle your answer.

a. It is my prediction that you will like this story very much.
b. It takes prediction to be able to write a good story.
c. You need to put the characters in an interesting prediction.
d. There needs to be exciting events and a happy prediction.

Day 4 predictable

1. How would you complete this sentence? Say it aloud to a partner.

I like things to be predictable because ______.

2. List three things that are *predictable* in your life.

a. ______________________________

b. ______________________________

c. ______________________________

3. Which phrase best completes this sentence? Circle your answer.

If someone is predictable, ______.

a. you never know what she will do
b. she always surprises you
c. you always know what to expect
d. she can tell you what the weather will be tomorrow

Day 5 expect • predict prediction • predictable

Fill in the bubble next to the correct answer.

1. If you expect something to happen, you ________.

Ⓐ are afraid that it won't happen
Ⓑ don't know that it will happen
Ⓒ have reason to believe that it will happen
Ⓓ have no idea when it will happen

2. Which sentence uses the word *predict* correctly?

Ⓕ Dora likes to predict she is a famous person.
Ⓖ Can you predict how many beans are in the jar?
Ⓗ Greg's little brother likes to predict he's a dog.
Ⓙ Can you predict how the story would end?

3. When you make a *prediction,* you ________.

Ⓐ figure out the answer to a problem
Ⓑ put events in the order in which they happen
Ⓒ tell what's going to happen before it does
Ⓓ don't understand what's going on

4. If a TV show is *predictable,* ________.

Ⓕ there are lots of surprises
Ⓖ you know what will happen next
Ⓗ it is probably about the past
Ⓙ you can't wait to see it again

Writing Make a *prediction* about something that will take place at school in the next few weeks. Be sure to use the word *prediction* in your writing.

____

____

____

REVIEW: Weeks 28–35

Daily Academic Vocabulary

approach	cooperation	judge	predict
conduct	expect	judgment	prove
content	feature	objective	

Day 1

Fill in the blanks with words from the word box.

You can't ________________ a book by its cover, but the cover can help you choose a book. The cover gives you hints about the book's ________________. Covers usually ________________ a brief summary of the book. It tells you what you can ________________. Then you can use your ________________ to decide if the book is one you will enjoy.

Day 2

Fill in the blanks with words from the word box.

Inquiry is the way that scientists ________________ answering scientific questions. First, they decide what they want to find out and set their goal or ________________. Next, they plan experiments and ________________ what the experiments will ________________ or disprove. Then, they ________________ the experiments and study the results. It often takes the ________________ of many scientists to discover new things.

REVIEW: Weeks 28–35

Daily Academic Vocabulary

assist	contents	labels	predictions	term
assistance	features	objects	purpose	view

Day 3

Fill in the blanks with words from the word box.

"Buddy Reading" is a ________________ for reading with a partner. A person who reads well reads with someone who is learning to read. The better reader gives ____________________ in figuring out words and their meanings. The buddies talk about the different ________________ of the story and make ________________ about what will happen. The ________________ of Buddy Reading is to help someone learn to read better.

Day 4

Fill in the blanks with words from the word box.

Mr. Cross is making a science lab in our classroom. He asked Serena to help and ________________ him. Mr. Cross is putting all the lab supplies in clear glass containers. That will make it easy to ________________ the ________________ of the containers. Serena is helping by making ________________ for the jars and for other ________________ used in the lab.

Day 5

Crossword Challenge

For each clue, write one of the words from the word box to complete the puzzle.

assist	**disprove**	**operate**	**process**
cooperate	**object**	**predictable**	**proof**

Down

1. to work together
3. happening in the way you expect
4. a series of actions that make something
5. facts that show something is true

Across

2. to work or run
6. to show that something is false
7. to help
8. something that can be seen